The Intellectual Crisis

in

American Public Administration

There is a paradox ... in the long
series of discussions over the theory of
bureaucracy. During the last fifty years,
many first-rate social scientists have thought
of bureaucracy as one of the key questions of
modern sociology and modern political science.
Yet the discussion about bureaucracy is still,
to a large extent, the domain of myths and
pathos of ideology.
On the one hand, most authors consider
the bureaucratic organization to be the
embodiment of rationality in the modern world,
and, as such to be intrinsically superior to
all other forms of human organization. On the
other hand, many authors—often the same
ones—consider it a sort of Leviathan,
preparing the enslavement of the human race.
This paradoxical view of bureaucracy in
Western thought has paralyzed positive
thinking ... and has favored the making of
catastrophic prognostications.

Michel Crozier, *The Bureaucratic Phenomenon.*

The Intellectual Crisis

in

American Public Administration

by

Vincent Ostrom

Revised Edition

THE UNIVERSITY OF ALABAMA PRESS
University, Alabama

For my Mother,
Alma Knudsen Ostrom,
who taught me my first
lessons in democratic theory.

1st Edition Copyright © *1973*
Revised Edition Copyright © *1974 by*
THE UNIVERSITY OF ALABAMA PRESS
ISBN 0-8173-4817-4
Library of Congress Catalog Card Number 73-38
All rights reserved
Manufactured in the United States of America

Preface

MANY YEARS OF TEACHING AND RESEARCH HAVE CON-
tributed to this effort to reconsider the intellectual foundations for both the study and practice of public administration. My graduate education in public administration
was in the traditional mainstream. Leonard White's *Introduction* was *the* basic text in my first introduction to the
subject.

While on the faculty at the University of Wyoming,
I became interested in the development of public organizations associated with water supply and land use in the
arid regions of the American West. I gave serious thought
to writing a dissertation on politics and grass as a study
of policy development in problems of public land management. When I decided to return to Los Angeles to begin
the dissertation, I shifted my focus to problems of water
policy in the development of Los Angeles and the southern
California metropolitan region.

The traditional theory of administration was not very
helpful in understanding the different forms of public
organization which were created to provide water supplies
and manage public lands in the arid West. The works
of John W. Powell, Elwood Mead, William Hammond

Hall, Frederick Jackson Turner, Walter Prescott Webb, and Samuel Wiel were more helpful.

At the University of Oregon, I became associate director of a Cooperation Program in Educational Administration for the Pacific Northwest region. The CPEA was funded by the W. K. Kellogg Foundation to improve graduate education in educational administration. Officials in the Kellogg Foundation, on the basis of experience in the field of medicine, drew the analogy that improvements in training educational administrators would depend upon better intellectual foundations in the social sciences in the same way that professional education in medicine had been based upon intellectual foundations in the biological science. My task was to work with colleagues in the social sciences to develop these intellectual foundations. This became an occasion for exploring a very wide range of literature related to public administration in anthropology, economics, psychology, and sociology, as well as in education and in political science.

This was the period when the debate engendered by Simon's challenge was at its peak. In my efforts to come to grasp with the issues that were then being discussed and debated, I found John Dewey, Mary Parker Follett, Chester I. Barnard, Homer Barnett, Harold Lasswell, Kurt Lewin, and Elton Mayo to be most useful in reformulating my thinking. Public administration became a form of problem solving writ large. Somehow problem solving, learning, epistemology, decision making, and organization were all threads from a common fabric.

Work with problems of educational administration fueled my scepticism regarding the traditional principles of public administration. The contention that independent school districts should be eliminated and integrated into a single general unit of local government was becoming less and less persuasive. Independent officials could collaborate as colleagues in a community without being subordinated to a single chief executive. Furthermore, the largest school systems were clearly not the "best." Somehow, a multiplicity of independent jurisdictions had not generated chaos. The American system of education had many surprisingly consistent patterns of organization in the absence of any overarching hierarchy of authority. No master-general of American education could look at his watch and know what lesson students in each school would be studying at any one moment.

Students, teachers, or school administrators could transfer from Maine to California and be required to make relatively small adjustments in pursuing their course of work in a new situation. Similarities in graduate education, rivalry for personnel through competitive placement offices, accrediting associations, professional associations of teachers, administrators, and school board members were a few of the institutions where consensus evolved from discussions of problems and possibilities. New ideas which offered the possibility of greater return for the effort were worth trying.

My work with the Kellogg project was interrupted by a year at the Center for Advanced Study in the Behavioral Sciences. This was an occasion for rethinking the intellectual foundations for political science and public administration. Problems raised by Dewey and by Lasswell led me off into analytical, historical, and comparative jurisprudence. Patterns of social organization are constituted by reference to decision rules. Somehow we needed to work with structures of legal relationships if we were to understand the architecture of organization. Llewellyn and Hoebel's *Cheyenne Way,* W. N. Hohfeld's *Fundamental Legal Conceptions,* and John R. Commons' *Legal Foundations of Capitalism* contributed important intellectual tools in this effort.

Residence at the Center also provided an opportunity to become acquainted with the work of W. R. Ashby.

[vii]

Ashby's *Design for a Brain* is essentially a theory of adaptive behavior which indeed enables one to comprehend problem solving, learning, epistemology, decision making, and organization as parts of a common fabric. Ashby's theory of adaptive behavior is today a basic foundation for my own work in political or organization theory.

The year at the Center and a Faculty Research Fellowship from the Social Science Research Council provided the occasion whereby I began to recognize the importance of economic theory for the study of public administration. I had become interested in bargaining as a decision process occurring among organizations in the public sector. Charles Lindblom's work on bargaining was a helpful beginning. The interest expanded to major proportions after I joined the faculty at UCLA and began a period of collaboration with Charles M. Tiebout, a political economist concerned with the provision of public goods and services by local governmental agencies. Our essay on "The Organization of Government in Metropolitan Areas: A Theoretical Inquiry" was a product of that effort. Studies by Robert Warren, Robert Bish, and Elinor Ostrom have since extended that analysis.

Further work in the political economy tradition was supported by Resources for the Future, Inc., for a study of the California water industry. My efforts to deal with patterns of organization in the California water industry are presented in a study for the National Water Commission on *Institutional Arrangements for Water Resource Development* (1971 b).

Without the opportunities afforded by support from the W. K. Kellogg Foundation, The Center for Advanced Study in the Behavioral Sciences, the Social Science Research Council, The National Water Commission, and Resources for the Future, Inc., I doubt that I would have been able to work my way through to an alternative approach to the study of public administration.

These essays are only a beginning that points in new directions while drawing upon a much older approach. The relationship of the new to the old is indicated by my essay on *The Political Theory of a Compound Republic* (1971a). In that essay I attempted to reconstruct the political theory inherent in *The Federalist* papers on the assumption that Alexander Hamilton and James Madison were political economists doing a policy analysis regarding a problem of governmental organization in 1787.

The format of a lecture series afforded by the Alabama lectures in public administration provided a most stimulating environment for exploring the intellectual crisis in American public administration. I am grateful to Professors Robert B. Highsaw and Coleman B. Ransone, Jr., for the opportunity to write these essays and present them in lecture form. I am especially appreciative of the students and faculty at the University of Alabama who carried on a lively discussion of the issues raised. It was a memorable experience for me.

I have also had the benefit of comments, criticisms, and suggestions from students and colleagues at Indiana University. Among those who helped by critiquing the first draft were Abdelrahmen Abdelrahmen, Kenneth Auerbach, Alfred Cuzan, Charles Kuhlman, Brian Loveman, Ronald Oakerson, Richard Plath, Sam Postbrief, Bruce Rogers, Philip Sabetti, Stephen Staub, George Stein, Dennis Smith, Michael Vlaisavljevich, Gordon Whitaker, Alfred Diamant, John Gillespie, Frank Hoole, Charles Hyneman, Elinor Ostrom, and Dina Zinnes. Alan Campbell, John Gallagher, Phillip Gregg, Dwight Waldo, and Donald Zauderer also made helpful comments on the first draft of these lectures. While I had the benefit of their help, I alone must assume responsibility for the defects which remain. I am also much indebted to Melanie Cloghessy, Deborah Davis, Pat Day, Madelyn Frohn, Dennis Gilliam, Pat Lee, and Mary Zielinski, who have helped in the preparation of manuscripts at one or another stage in its development.

The circumstance of a sabbatical leave at Indiana University gave me a flexible schedule for a writing program. The Office of Research and Advanced Studies at Indiana University has been generous in providing a small but essential budget in support of my research efforts. I am much indebted to Indiana University for this assistance.

VINCENT OSTROM
Bloomington, Indiana
February, 1972

PREFATORY NOTE TO REVISED EDITION

The intellectual crisis considered in these lectures has become the basis of a major constitutional crisis over executive authority. A postscript on "Watergate and the Constitutional Crisis of the 1970's" has been added. The traditional prescriptions for administrative reform are yielding a bitter harvest.

No substantive changes have been made in the text of chapters 1–5. The notes, list of references, and index have been enlarged to reflect the addition of the postscript.

VINCENT OSTROM
November, 1973

Contents

III
THE WORK OF THE CONTEMPORARY POLITICAL ECONOMISTS

IV
A THEORY OF DEMOCRATIC ADMINISTRATION: THE REJECTED ALTERNATIVE

V

THE CHOICE OF ALTERNATIVE FUTURES

POSTSCRIPT
WATERGATE AND THE CONSTITUTIONAL
CRISIS OF THE 1970'S

The Intellectual Crisis

in

American Public Administration

The Crisis of Confidence

Introduction

AS WE APPROACH THE BICENTENARY OF AMERICAN NATION-
hood, we are losing confidence that the twenty-first century will be an American century (Hacker, 1970). Instead,
we have been seized by a maelstrom of crises. Some have
even begun to wonder whether there will be a twenty-first
century in the Christian era, and whether the United
States of America will survive as a nation.

Whatever fate or destiny the future may hold for human
civilization, that future will be a product of human choice.
Technical capabilities now exist for human beings to
choose a fate marking the end of modern civilization as
we know it. Today, the choice to destroy much of mankind
can be made by a mere handful of men. If that choice
is ever made, we can be reasonably confident that Americans acting in "the line of duty" will have participated
in that fateful decision. Such a decision can, indeed, be
taken with considerable "speed and dispatch" and with
relatively small expenditures of "time and effort" in decision making.

The range of possibilities which are today at the command of human choice far exceeds those available to prior generations. But a wealth of possibilities always interposes proportionately higher decision costs. The more benign the future of this civilization, the more time and effort will be required in fashioning decision structures appropriate to human creativity, and the less we can afford to rely upon preemptive strategies involving speed and dispatch. The course of destruction is simple; the course of constructive action is much more complex and difficult.

If the practice of public administration is based upon a knowledge of the organizational terms and conditions which are necessary to advance human welfare, then those of us who teach public administration should be able to indicate what those terms and conditions are. In short, we should be able to specify the consequences which will follow from different organizational conditions. To assert that consequences follow from conditions is to say that effects have their causes. Knowledge depends upon the specification of relationships between conditions and consequences, between causes and effects. We should be able to indicate the conditions and consequences which derive from the choice of alternative organizational arrangements if theories of organization have scientific warrantability. (See Meehan, 1971.)

If we have a body of knowledge that enables us to estimate the probable consequences evoked by different organizational arrangements, we should then be able to pursue two forms of analysis. One form of analysis uses theory to draw inferences about consequences to be anticipated. These inferences can be used as hypotheses to guide empirical research and test the predictive value of theory. If theory has predictive value for indicating consequences which can be expected to flow from specifiable structural conditions, then we can have some measure of confidence in that theory.

A second form of analysis derives from the first. When relationships between conditions and consequences can be specified and when any particular set of consequences is judged to be detrimental to human welfare, we should then be able to specify the conditions which lead to that set of consequences. Consequences of organizational arrangements which are detrimental to human welfare can be viewed as social pathologies. If the conditions leading to those pathologies can be specified, then the basis exists for diagnosing the organizational conditions of social pathologies. If conditions can be altered so as to evoke a different set of consequences, then different forms of remedial action can be considered. By altering the appropriate conditions, one set of consequences judged to be pathological might be avoided and another set of consequences judged to be more benign might be realized.

The relationships that I have just specified indicate the connection between theory and practice in the use of any body of knowledge. The practice of any *profession* depends upon the knowledge which its members *profess*. The worth of professional practice depends upon the difference that professional advice will make in the opportunities which are made available to those who rely upon that advice. If I seek professional advice and that advice either reduces the misery that I would otherwise have suffered or improves the advantage that I might realize, then such advice is of value to me. If, on the other hand, professional advice leaves me worse off, I would have to conclude that such advice is harmful.

Organizational arrangements can be thought of as nothing more or less than decision-making arrangements. Decision-making arrangements establish the terms and conditions for making choices. Consequently, we would expect that the practice of public administration will increase in importance as the domain of choice is extended to include an increasing range of opportunities. I doubt that there are many today who anticipate a decline in the relative importance of the practice of public administration so long as opportunities exist for continued advancement in human welfare.

We are, however, confronted with a substantial question of whether the bodies of knowledge used by those who practice public administration will lead toward an improvement in or an erosion of human welfare. If, perchance, the consequence of acting upon knowledge used in the practice of public administration were a decline in human welfare, we would have to conclude that such knowledge contributes to social pathologies. Conventional wisdom in public administration indicates, for example, that efficiency will be enhanced by eliminating overlapping jurisdictions and fragmentation of authority. What, for example, would be the consequence of eliminating eighty per cent of the units of local government in the United States? (Committee for Economic Development, 1966.) Would the consequence of such action substantially enhance or diminish human welfare? We could hardly expect such action to be *without* consequences.

Dare we contemplate the possibility that the contemporary malaise in American society may have been derived, in part, from the teachings of public administration? The consolidation or merger of units of local government has, in some cases, attained substantial success. Have those successes been congruent with the consequences which we expected? Is New York City a model of what we would like to achieve? Or, has it become a gargantuan system which is virtually ungovernable? If our teachings have contributed to the contemporary malaise, we might further contemplate the possibility that continued reliance upon those teachings, as the basis for prescribing remedies to contemporary social pathologies, can lead to further deteriorations in human welfare.

If such a circumstance prevails, we are confronted with a growing dilemma. On the one hand, the practice of public administration will increase in relative significance. But as it grows in importance, we would see those affected by public administration to be confronted with a progressively deteriorating situation. Actions taken to remedy conditions would exacerbate problems. In such a circumstance, we might expect to find that those educated in public administration were no more successful in the practice of public administration than those who were not educated for the practice of that profession. They might be even less successful than others not so educated.

Perhaps, this is an occasion where we should entertain an outlandish hypothesis: that our teachings include much bad medicine. This is a conclusion which I have reached after considerable agonizing about the problem. I once had hoped that I could be proved wrong. I have since abandoned that hope; and I have attempted to work my way through to alternative solutions. I am now persuaded that the major task in the next decade will be to lay new foundations for the study of public administration. If these foundations are well laid over the next decade, we should see a new political science join the new economics in establishing the basis for a major new advance upon the frontiers of public administration.

The Persistent Crisis in the Study of Public Administration

When I was first introduced to the study of public administration on the eve of World War II, the confidence reflected in the theory and practice of public administration impressed me. The theory of administration presumed that technical solutions were available to public problems. Once decisions specifying policy objectives were reached, we assumed that the translation of these objectives into social realities was a technical problem within the competence of professional administrative expertise. The social problems associated with the Great Depression were transformed into new programs by enlightened political leadership and the technical proficiency of those who staffed the public service. Students in the late 1930's displayed as much enthusiasm for the Public Service as many of their counterparts now have for The Movement.

Perhaps the high point of that era was reflected in the publication of the *Report* (1937) of the President's Committee on Administrative Management and the companion volume edited by Luther Gulick and L. Urwick as *Papers on the Science of Administration* (1937). The *Papers* stated the theoretical foundations for the science of administration. The *Report* proposed a bold new reorganization plan based upon that science of administration to rationalize the host of New Deal agencies into a coherent administrative structure.

The war years provoked a challenge from which the study of public administration has never recovered. Wartime control measures were plagued by persistent failures.[1] Public administration sometimes appeared to involve greater measures of unprincipled expediency than of principled action. The principles of administrative organization were honored more in their breach than by their observance. The gap between theory and practice became increasingly difficult to bridge.

The wartime experiences with civil and military administration were more congruent with the work of Elton Mayo and his colleagues (Mayo, 1933) in the Western Electric experiment than with the work of Urwick and Gulick. The human relations aspect of organization appeared to have a greater effect on productivity than formal tables of organization. The gulf between theory and practice was, indeed, formalized by distinguishing between a theory of formal organization and a theory of informal organization.

Perhaps the most devastating blow came in the carefully reasoned analysis sustained by Herbert Simon in his study of *Administrative Behavior*. Simon explicitly rejected the principles of public administration as little more than proverbs (Simon, 1946; Simon, 1947: 20–44.) Like proverbs, Simon concluded upon analysis that the traditional principles of public administration could be arrayed into logically contradictory sets. One or another principle could always be invoked to justify contradictory positions.

The central thrust of Simon's challenge has never been effectively faulted. Considerable debate was engendered by his fact-value distinction. His call for an administrative science was widely supported. His organization theory was different but not unfamiliar.

Many of us who lived through the era following Simon's challenge found ourselves in basic agreement with a number of his contentions. At other points we sustained serious reservations. For example, many of us have been concerned with Simon's use of the fact-value distinction to dichotomize policy and administration. (Simon, 1947: 52–59.) In addition, some have had a sense that Simon did not go far enough: that his theoretical thrust implied much more than he developed.

Leonard White in the third edition of his *Introduction to the Study of Public Administration,* for example, reviewed Simon's contention that the rule implied by unity of command was logically incompatible with the rule implied by specialization in technical competencies. White, however, was able to demonstrate that:

[7]

Simon eventually grants priority to the rule of unity of command but reformulates the proposition in these words: 'In case two authoritative commands conflict, there should be a single determinate person whom the subordinate is expected to obey; and the sanctions of authority should be applied against the subordinate only to enforce his obedience to that one person.' (White, 1948:38.)

Somehow, the thrust of Simon's theoretical criticisms should have generated a far less conventional conclusion. Perhaps this observation applies to all of us: that the extent of our theoretical doubts should lead to far less conventional inquiries than we are willing to pursue.

By a curious coincidence, the translated works of Max Weber were published in America at the same time that Herbert Simon's *Administrative Behavior* first made its appearance. (Gerth and Mills, 1946; Parsons, 1947.) Max Weber's works on *Economy and Society* were a powerful effort to fashion a general sociological theory based upon what he presumed to be a value-free approach to the study of social phenomena. In formulating his general sociology, Max Weber established certain ideal types to define social structures which functioned as elements in the organization of societies. Weber conceived a hierarchically ordered system of public administration, which he identified as "bureaucracy," to be one of the necessary organizational requisites for a modern society. Bureaucracy provided a rational basis for social organization. Weber's theory of bureaucracy became an important influence upon work both in the sociology of large-scale organization and in public administration during the post World War II era.

Weber's commitment to a value-free social science was fully congruent with Simon's fact-value position. His concept of bureaucracy was offered as an ideal type to be used as a measure analogous to a well-calibrated yardstick. Weber's conception of bureaucracy would, thus, serve as a model which scholars could use in arraying imperfect cases of human organization. Weber's theory of bureaucracy was fully congruent with the traditional theory of public administration in both form and method.

In this circumstance, the postwar challenge to the traditional approach to public administration was accompanied by a new intellectual thrust that tended to reinforce traditional commitments of American scholarship in public administration. Woodrow Wilson and his contemporaries, such as Frank J. Goodnow, drew their inspiration for the study of public administration from French and German scholarship concerned with highly centralized bureaucratic structures. Weber, whose lifework was largely contemporary with Wilson's, provided a powerful restatement of that theory of administrative organization. The very theory that was being challenged by Simon was at the same time being reinforced and sustained by Weber, one of the twentieth century's most powerful social theorists. A theory challenged in one context reappeared in the cloak of different words and phrases to realize a new era of splendor.

The ambiguities of the shifting theoretical scene were accompanied by shifting styles of work in scholarly research. Early research in public administration had been management-oriented. Typically, such research included reference to organization, planning, budgeting, personnel and selected aspects of program operation. The empirical thrust was diagnostic in character. Conclusions were usually accompanied by policy recommendations congruent with the prevailing theory of public administration.

The wartime experiences of many of the students of public administration led to a new style of research reflected in case studies designed to provide a narrative about the "realities" of administrative decision making. (Stein, 1952.) Case studies dramatized issues and pointed to the pervasiveness of conflict within the administrative setting. Case studies were used extensively as teaching materials to give students a sense of "reality" about administration. In the absence of a reformulation of administrative theory, these "realities" become increasingly incongruent with theory.

Still another research tradition was stimulated by students of administration who came to adopt the behavioral approach and its commitment to building theory by generating and testing hypotheses. Theory, the behavioralists hoped, might gradually evolve from the accumulation of tested hypotheses. The work of the behavioral scientists became an important contributor to the challenge to traditional theory. Emphasis upon goal displacement and bureaucratic dysfunctions appeared in much of the behavioral research and reinforced the prevailing doubts about bureaucratic rationality. (Merton, 1952; Blau, 1956; March and Simon, 1958; Crozier, 1964.) The strategy of the bureaucratic personality who followed the rule of thumb, "when in doubt, don't," stood in sharp contrast to the presumptions of efficiency, speed, and dispatch which Weber had attributed to bureaucratic organization. (Merton, 1952:378.) The new research strategies which developed in light of the wartime and postwar challenge to the theory of public administration merely served to deepen and to reinforce the challenge.

By late 1967, Dwight Waldo was able to characterize the crisis of confidence in public administration as a crisis of identity. According to Waldo,

> *Both the nature and boundaries of the subject matter and the methods of studying and teaching this subject matter became problematical. Now, two decades after the critical attacks, the crisis of identity has not been resolved satisfactorily. Most of the important theoretical problems of public administration relate to this continuing crisis, to ways in*

which it can be resolved and to the implications and results of possible resolutions. (Waldo, 1968:5.   Waldo's emphasis.)

Waldo is pessimistic about the resolution of this identity crisis—this failure to know what we are (subject matter) or how we should proceed (methods). Indeed, he concludes that there is no solution to the problem at the level at which it was originally posed. The crisis, he contends, cannot be resolved by a choice between the alternatives presented in the traditional theory and in Simon's challenge. Both have proved wanting: neither is viable. The search for a solution must occur outside the frame of reference provided by either the traditional theory of public administration, or Simon's theory of organization.

Waldo's proposal for a short-term solution pending a longer-term resolution of the identity crisis is as follows:

What I propose is that we try to act as a profession without actually being one and perhaps even without the hope or intention of becoming one in any strict sense. (Waldo, 1968:10, Waldo's emphasis.)

Waldo then goes on to observe, "Frankly, it took some courage to say that, as it is patently open to ridicule." Waldo's advice is indeed open to ridicule. It is the advice of a friend who at a time of overwhelming tragedy counsels that one should keep a stiff upper lip.

If the methods of studying, teaching, and practicing the subject matter of public administration have become problematical, then that profession can*not* have much confidence in what it professes. The practice of a profession rests upon the validity of the knowledge which it professes.[2] When the confidence of a profession in the essential validity of its knowledge has been shattered, that profession should be extraordinarily modest about the

[11]

professional advice it renders while keeping up its appearances.

Waldo's proposal has a fatal flaw if practitioners in the profession of public administration render professional advice when they do not know the grounds upon which their advice is predicated. In an era of political turmoil when everyone is being challenged to demonstrate the relevance of his knowledge to the solution of pressing social problems, it is difficult, if not impossible, I fear, to profess modesty and doubt.

The nature of the flaw is emphasized by a recent announcement that the American Society for Public Administration has established a Task Force on Society Goals. The announcement is somewhat ambiguous as to whether the term "Society" in Society Goals refers to ASPA, the USA, or even more broadly to human society in general. Let me read a few sentences from the announcement to indicate the problem.

> Today's crisis exceeds all historical crises in public administration . . .. Public executives, taken as a group, have not yet awakened to the fact that they are in charge. They are responsible for the operation of our society; they cannot wait around for someone to tell them what to do. If they don't know, we're lost.[3]

From such a statement one might observe that exuberance for action need not be limited by the fact that men know not what they do. Times are critical. We rush to meet crises with calls for urgency and fears of impending disaster.

In view of these circumstances the first order of priority in the study of public administration is to come to grasp with the crisis of confidence—the identity crisis—that has clouded work in the field for the last generation. I am persuaded that we can begin to take important steps leading toward a resolution of this crisis of identity. This is the issue which I will address during these lectures on *The Intellectual Crisis in American Public Administration.*

The Crisis as a Paradigm Problem

A first step in proceeding toward a resolution is to diagnose our crisis of identity as a recurrent problem in the history of scientific inquiry. Thomas S. Kuhn in a study of *The Structure of Scientific Revolutions* provides us with a useful analysis. Kuhn, as a historian of science, distinguishes between the practice of normal science and of the extraordinary science associated with scientific revolutions.

The essential characteristic of normal science is general agreement upon a basic theoretical paradigm or framework in which a community of scholars shares common theoretical assumptions, and a common language defining essential terms and relationships. The "agreement" upon an underlying paradigm is usually an implicit agreement. Each scholar takes it for granted in the organization and conduct of his work. Methods of work, conceptions of what is problematical, and criteria for what is to be included or excluded from the field of inquiry follow from a theoretical paradigm. The basic concepts and assumptions in a theory establish the defining sets and determine what is to be included and what is to be excluded from a scholar's frame of analysis. They tell the scholar what to "take hold of" in the conduct of his inquiry.

The basic concepts establish the essential elements of analysis; and relational postulates and axioms specify the essential rules of reason. These rules of reason enable members of an intellectual community to pursue a structure of inferential reasoning where the work of one can be added to the work of others. Frontiers of knowledge can be extended with reference to the understanding shared by all members of the community.

[13]

When general agreement on a paradigm prevails, scholars work within the confines of that framework pursuing inquiry into a range of problems inferred or suggested by the paradigm. As long as work proceeds with a reasonably good fit between expectations and occurrences, scholarship is advanced in a step by step fashion. Normal science proceeds in a cumulative way in which bits and pieces are added to the frontier of knowledge by those who work within a prevailing community of scholarship.

However, Kuhn contends that probing into new problems, inherent in the method of normal science, can evoke anomalous consequences which deviate radically from expectations. Such anomalies cannot be satisfactorily explained within the traditional framework. As those anomalies persist, the theoretical paradigm will itself come into question. When that happens, a crisis occurs for the community of scholars. The common understanding which provided the bond of community is beclouded with doubt. Scientific work shifts from the application of the prevailing paradigm to new problems, and turns back to questioning the sufficiency of the theoretical framework itself.

During a period of paradigmatic crisis, a proliferation of competing articulations of the prevailing paradigm will occur. As the common bond of understanding is relaxed by contentions over the prevailing paradigm, members of a scholarly community will be more random in their choice of research strategies. Methodological experimentation will also be accompanied by debates over basic philosophical and epistemological issues. The doubts, methodological experiments, and philosophical debates lead to explicit expressions of discontent and unhappiness. When these characteristics prevail, a community of scholars is experiencing an intellectual crisis. The theoretical framework which provided the common bond of understanding has itself become problematical.

The process of normal science ends in crisis. The stage for scientific revolutions occurs within this background of crisis. When the proliferation of alternative versions of the traditional theory has failed to resolve the prevailing crisis, a radically different formulation is needed. But the more radical the reformulation, the less will be the common basis for making a choice between a traditional paradigm, its numerous variations, and a new, more revolutionary, paradigm.

A new paradigm implies that a different form of basic ABC's is required for thinking about a subject matter. New concepts, different terms, and different postulates will give rise to a different pattern in inferential reasoning among the community of scholars and professional practitioners associated with that field of study. Scholarship which qualified and modified the old ABC's will be insufficient because the basic structure of thought was unsatisfactory. A new ABC's needs to be considered as a possible substitute for the old ABC's.

Sophisticated scholars in the old tradition will view efforts to reconstruct the logic inherent in the old ABC's as resurrecting a "dead horse." Those old ideas have been critically scrutinized over and over again. But it is the old ABC's that need replacing. A new qualification or a new extension in their use will not resolve the intellectual crisis.

The setting for revolutionary change occurs when none of the alternative versions of the traditional theory has succeeded in resolving the issues created by the anomalies generated in the course of prior work. The process of scientific revolution itself can begin only *after* an alternative paradigm has been articulated to a point where it is perceived to be an alternative. The alternative itself may not be appropriately stated in its early forms. Thus, the process of scientific revolution may be a prolonged one. The Copernican revolution in astronomy, for example, covered a period of more than a century.

The articulation of an alternative paradigm is, however, a necessary condition before a scientific revolution can occur. Scientific revolutions require a choice among alternative paradigms. If Kuhn's theory of scientific revolutions is valid, we can anticipate a resolution of the intellectual crisis in public administration only if an alternative paradigm is available. If a new paradigm is to succeed, it must offer a formulation that is able to resolve some of the persisting anomalies and be able to provide an explanation which would take account of the prior attainments by scholars working in the earlier tradition. A new paradigm might also be expected to open new horizons to research. The new formulation may allow for the conception of relationships such that problems previously excluded from inquiry are now perceived to have an ordered relevance to the previously defined field of inquiry. In addition, a new paradigm may permit a greater precision in explanation and in measurement. These considerations involve potential gains which might be realized from the development of a new paradigm.

These potential gains need, however, to be viewed in light of potential losses. A change in paradigm is likely to require the abandonment of previously held beliefs, specialized language, and methodological tools and skills acquired in the practice associated with those beliefs. Retooling is a costly process. As long as prevailing tools appear to work in solving problems, then we would expect scholars to take advantage of those opportunities which remain available to them. We would not expect scholars to abandon lightly their prior investment in skills and tools without anticipating a payoff which would justify the added expenditure of time and effort to acquire a new way for approaching one's field of study and developing new methods of work.

The more radical the revolution, the fewer the commensurabilities that will exist between the old and the new. The degree of incommensurability which we might expect to find can be estimated by reference to the constitutive effect of a paradigm. If there is a shift in basic organizing concepts, we would want to know whether the new will take account of the old and simultaneously take account of at least some of the prior anomalies. If there is a change in the basic unit of analysis, then scholars may be required to "take hold of" their subject in quite a different way. The basic assumptions may imply quite different boundary conditions for estimating the essential relevance or irrelevance of the larger universe of events. The relational postulates and axioms may imply quite a different structure of reasoning about the subject. A scholar may have to approach his subject in a different way and view it from quite different perspectives. Finally, the horizon viewed from a new perspective may include many unfamiliar features as well as some familiar landmarks which now appear in a new context. It is even faintly possible that the beauties of a yesteryear may be revealed as ugly illusions; and some of those obscure figures in the background may shine with a new brilliance.

The Paradigm Problem in Public Administration

In the course of these lectures, I shall advance the thesis that the sense of crisis which has pervaded the field of public administration over the last generation is a crisis evoked by the insufficiency of the paradigm inherent in the traditional theory of public administration. Simon's challenge will be viewed as a challenge to the traditional theory of public administration based upon a number of anomalies inherent in that traditon. The study of public administration during the postwar period is one which has all the characteristics that Kuhn associates with a paradigmatic crisis.

Kuhn's own work was concerned with the physical sciences of astronomy, physics, and chemistry. Yet the study of public administration during this period of crisis has been characterized by the proliferation of numerous versions of the prevailing theory, by the willingness of scholars to engage in methodological experimentation, by the expression of explicit discontent, by recourse to philosophical speculation, and by debate over fundamental epistemological issues. These are Kuhn's symptoms of crisis.

I agree with Waldo's conclusion that the resolution of the crisis cannot be attained by a choice between the traditional theory of administration and Simon's theory of organization. Simon's theory was essentially cast within the same mold as the traditional theory of administration. It was an alternative articulation of the old theoretical paradigm. Neither is a viable alternative.

Simon's effort to reconstruct organization theory made a number of critical breaks with tradition. His reconstruction gave a new emphasis to the psychology of decision making and to considerations bearing upon a model of organization man. His formulation of the criterion of efficiency proposed the application of a cost calculus which would allow for an independent test of efficiency other than presuming the efficiency of bureaucratic structures. Prior to his work on *Administrative Behavior,* Simon did pioneering work on measuring the output of public service agencies. (Ridley and Simon, 1938; Simon, Divine, Cooper and Chernin, 1941.) He conceived a solution to the problem of identifying and measuring the output of public agencies as necessary to a rational theory of public administration. (Simon, 1947:189.) However, his subsequent work has been preoccupied with a different range of problems. (Simon, 1965; Simon, 1969.)

[18]

The principal efforts to conceptualize and define social production functions has instead been pursued by political economists in work on externalities, common properties, and the theory of public goods. Based upon a theory of public goods, these political economists are developing a theory of collective action which assumes that the principles of organization required for the efficient conduct of *public* enterprises will be different from the principles of organization for private enterprises. Competition among private enterprises in a market structure will tend to regulate activities among firms without regard for the structural characteristics of any particular firm. In the absence of a product market where a consumer is not free to choose among alternatives, public enterprises must provide complex political decision-making arrangements for translating individual preferences into collective choices regarding the provision of public goods and services. The constitution of public enterprises will thus make for significant differences in the way consumer preferences are translated into the provision of public goods and services.[4] These differences emphasize what would be traditionally identified as the *political* aspects of public administration.

The theory of *public goods* is the central organizing concept used by these political economists in conceptualizing the problem of collective action and of public administration. This contrasts with the theory of *bureaucracy* as the central concept in the traditional theory of public administration. When the central problem in public administration is viewed as the provision of public goods and services, alternative forms of organization may be available for the performance of those functions apart from an extension and perfection of bureaucratic structures. Bureaucratic structures are necessary but not sufficient structures for a productive and responsive public service economy. Particular types of public goods and ser-

[19]

vices may be jointly provided by the coordinated actions of a multiplicity of enterprises transcending the limits of particular governmental jurisdictions. Some of these multi-organizational arrangements may take on characteristics analogous to industries composed of many different governmental agencies. Can we best understand the structure, conduct, and performance of the American system of higher education, for example, by reference to a bureaucratic chain of command accountable to a central chief executive or by reference to a relatively open but constrained rivalry among a diversity of collective enterprises?

In these lectures I shall be primarily concerned with revealing the underlying logic inherent in each theoretical paradigm. Logic is an important tool which enables us to draw plausible inferences from postulated conditions. When postulated conditions approximate the conditions of the empirical world, we can test inferences derived from theory by whether those inferences enable us to anticipate or predict the consequences which flow from specified conditions. (See Meehan, 1971.)

A danger always exists that theories may proliferate to such an extent that reasoning through logical inferences is abandoned and replaced by a process of naming different theories and writing narratives about theory. The study of theory then can become little more than interesting stories about the lives, loves and miscellaneous thoughts of political philosophers or the quaintness of different sets of ideas. We spend a great deal of time *talking about* theory and surprisingly little effort in the *use* of political theory. Scholars should know how to *use* theory and to *do* theory, not just *talk* about theory.

The next two lectures will be devoted to a clarification of each of the alternative approaches. In the second lecture of this series, I shall examine the traditional theory of public administration. I shall use Woodrow Wilson's work to state the basic argument. I shall then review Max Weber's theory of bureaucracy as an independent formulation similar to the classical theory. I shall then turn in particular to Luther Gulick's "Notes on the Theory of Organization."(1937) Surprisingly, it is Gulick's analysis that destroys the integrity of the traditional theory. However, he patched over the wreckage with an incantation of appropriate words and phrases as though he were reaffirming the faith. The task of explicitly challenging the faith was reserved for Simon. The alternative paradigm inherent in the work of the contemporary political economists will be examined in the third lecture.

These two approaches can provide alternative constructs for viewing the experiential world of public administration. An intellectual construct is like a pair of spectacles. We see and order events in the world by looking through our spectacles and constructs. We are apt to neglect a critical examination of the spectacles or constructs themselves. As Stephen Toulmin has observed, "We shall understand the merits of our ideas, instead of taking them for granted, only if we are prepared to look at these alternatives on their own terms." (Toulmin, 1961:102.)

In the fourth lecture, on "Democratic Administration," I shall use the spectacles of the political economists to reflect upon the paradigmatic choice made by Wilson when he rejected the "literary theories" and "paper pictures" used by Alexander Hamilton and James Madison in *The Federalist*. The theoretical paradigm of the contemporary political economists enables us to find a theory of administration in Hamilton's essays on taxation and defense which is a more general theory of administration than his theory of the national executive contained in *Federalist* 70 and 72. Alexis de Tocqueville drew upon a comparable political theory when he compared the patterns of democratic administration in America with the patterns of bureaucratic administration in France. Tocqueville's theory and empirical findings are congruent with the work of the contemporary political economists.

Finally, in my concluding lecture I shall focus upon the implications that these two different theoretical approaches have for the study and practice of public administration. If different ways for conceptualizing administrative arrangements are available, then different concepts may serve as a basis for the design of different organizational arrangements. New designs may, in turn, provide new remedies for some of our contemporary problems in public affairs. Perhaps, we can begin to contemplate how these new remedies might affect the future. If we believe that the new remedies will be an improvement over the old we may be confronted with a task of reformulating the study and practice of public administration. Perhaps there are alternatives to some of our contemporary crises.

The Intellectual Mainstream
In American Public Administration

Wilson's Point of Departure

THE BEGINNING OF MODERN INQUIRY IN AMERICAN PUBLIC administration is often identified with Woodrow Wilson's essay on "The Study of Administration" published in 1887. Frank J. Goodnow's *Politics and Administration* (1900) is another important statement of the classical theory of administration which is highly congruent with Wilson's formulation. In this discussion I shall rely upon Wilson's essay and his book on *Congressional Government* (1885) for an analysis of the theoretical foundations of American scholarship in public administration.

I do not wish to imply that the theory was original with Wilson and that others consciously followed in his footsteps. Rather, I assume that Wilson used an approach which he found helpful in his work, and that this approach was shared by other scholars who undertook graduate study in the newly organized departments of political science during the late nineteenth century. Many scholars in succeeding generations have, in turn, gone back to Wilson's work and found affirmation and inspiration for their own work. (E.g.: Caldwell, 1965; Dimock, 1937; Millett, 1959; Wengert, 1942; White, 1948.)

WILSON'S THEORETICAL PRESUMPTIONS

Wilson's choice of where to "take hold" of his subject is best formulated in *Congressional Government* (1885). The essential concern of a political scientist, according to Wilson, is to reveal "the real depositories and the essential machinery of power." Wilson's basic "reality" in politics rests on the assumption that "there is always *a* centre of power..." within any system of government. (My emphasis.) The task of the scholar is to identify 1) "where in this system is that centre?" 2) "in whose hands is [this] self-sufficient authority lodged?" 3) "through what agencies does that authority speak and act?" (Wilson, 1885:30.) Once the center for the exercise of sovereign prerogative is identified, then the structure of authority can be unravelled and the symmetry of social life in that political community can be understood.

Scholars must be prepared to penetrate the facade of political forms and focus upon the essential realities of power. The "literary theory" of the American Constitution, according to Wilson, was based upon "a balance of powers and a nice adjustment of interactive checks" which deny the presumption of a single controlling force in American politics. This was the facade, the "literary theory," or the "paper picture" of the American political system. (Wilson, 1885:31.)

But, what are the realities in the practical conduct of government? Wilson's central thesis in *Congressional Government* is a response to that question: "The predominant and controlling force, the centre and the source of all motive and all regulative power, is Congress." (Wilson, 1885:31.) He then goes on to observe:

[24]

All niceties of constitutional restriction and even many broad principles of constitutional limitations have been overridden, and a thoroughly organized system of congressional control was set up which gives a *very rude negative* to some theories of balance and some schemes for distributed power, but which suits well with convenience and does violence to none of the principles of self-government contained in the Constitution. (Wilson, 1885:31 My emphasis.)

Throughout his analysis in *Congressional Government,* Wilson recognized that the forms inherent in the "literary theory" of the American constitutional system did have substantial significance for political practice. The checks and balances created impediments to a smooth and harmonious relationship among the various decision structures within the American system of government. To drive his point home, Wilson observed that *"those checks and balances have proved mischievous just to the extent to which they have succeeded in establishing themselves as realities."* (Wilson, 1885:187. My emphasis.)

The central axiom in Wilson's political theory is the proposition that "the more power is divided the more irresponsible it becomes."[1] (Wilson, 1885:77.) Wilson's model for political organization was the British parliamentary system. "The natural, the inevitable tendency of every system of self-government like our own and the British," Wilson observes, "is to exalt the representative body, the people's parliament, to a position of absolute supremacy." (Wilson, 1885:203.) The forces of reality were leading the Americans to adjust sovereignty accordingly. "The plain tendency," that Wilson saw:

is toward a centralization of all the greater powers of government in the hands of federal authorities, and toward the practical confirmation of these *prerogatives of supreme overlordship* which Congress has been gradually arrogating to itself. The central government is constantly becoming stronger and more active, and Congress is establishing itself as the *one sovereign authority* in that government. (Wilson, 1885:205. My emphasis.)

Once the principle is accepted that the representatives of the people are the proper ultimate authority in all matters of government, then the originating and controlling force in the politics of a nation resides in its legislative body. It determines what shall be done; and the executive "is plainly bound in duty to render *unquestioning* obedience to Congress." (Wilson, 1885:181. My emphasis.) Those who fix the policies that the administration is to serve should be strictly accountable to the choice of the majority. Beyond that, "the conditions of self-government requires that a sharp line of distinction" be made "between those offices which are political and those which are *non*-political." (Wilson's emphasis.) "The strictest rules of business discipline, of merit tenure and earned promotion, must rule every office whose incumbent has not to do with choosing between policies...." (Wilson, 1885:190.)

WILSON'S THEORY OF ADMINISTRATION

Wilson's theory of administration is based upon this "sharp line of distinction" between "politics" and "administration." He defines politics as the enactment of public law, as the formulation of public policy. (Wilson, 1887:198 and 212.) Public administration is defined as the detailed and systematic execution of public law. (Wilson, 1887:212.) Governments may differ in the political principles underlying their constitutions; but principles of good administration are much the same in any system of government. That there is "... but one rule of good administration for all governments alike" is the basic thesis in Wilson's theory of administration. (Wilson, 1887:202.)[2]

The science of administration, according to Wilson, was most fully developed by French and German scholars at the turn of the century. (Wilson, 1887:202.) The practice of administration was most highly perfected in Prussia under Frederick the Great and Frederick William III and in France under Napoleon. (Wilson, 1887:204-205.) Monarchies and democracies may differ with respect to the political structures of their constitutions, but their administrative systems operate upon the same technical principles. (Wilson, 1887:218.)

> When we study the administrative systems of France and Germany, knowing that we are not in search of *political* principles, we need not care a peppercorn for the constitutional and political reasons which Frenchmen and Germans give for their practices when explaining them to us.... [I]f I see a monarchist died in the wool, I can learn his business methods without changing one of my republican spots. (Wilson, 1887:220. Wilson's emphasis.)

Wilson's thesis that there is "but one rule of good administration for all governments alike" carries two correlative implications. First, a theory or science of public administration is applicable to all political regimes; and second, a theory of administration is a general theory as distinct from the limited theories inherent in the ideological preoccupations of political theorists. Administration is an invariant relationship in all systems of government; and, thus, a science of administration has universal applicability to all political systems. Wilson could conceive of a theory of democratic government but *not* a theory of *democratic administration*.

Wilson also sustains the conclusion that modernity[3] in human civilization is associated with the perfection of a system of "good" administration. (Wilson, 1887:204.) A system of "good" administration will be hierarchically ordered in a system of graded ranks subject to political direction by heads of departments at the center of government. The ranks of administration will be filled by a corps of technically trained civil servants "prepared by a special schooling and drilled, after appointment, into a perfected organization, with an appropriate hierarchy and characteristic discipline. . . ." (Wilson, 1887:216.) Perfection in administrative organization is attained in a hierarchically ordered and professionally trained public service. Efficiency is attained by perfection in the hierarchical ordering of a professionally trained public service. Wilson also conceptualizes efficiency in economic terms: "the utmost possible efficiency and at the least possible cost of either money or of energy." (Wilson, 1887:197.) Thus, perfection in hierarchical ordering will maximize efficiency as measured by least cost expended in money or effort in realizing policy objectives.

BASIC PROPOSITIONS IN THE WILSONIAN PARADIGM

The basic propositions inherent in the paradigm that Wilson proposed to use in building a science of administration can be summarized as follows:

1. There will always be a single dominant center of power in any system of government; and the government of a society will be controlled by that single center of power.
2. The more power is divided the more irresponsible it becomes; or, alternatively, the more power is unified and directed from a single center the more responsible it will become.
3. The structure of a constitution defines and determines the composition of that center of power and establishes the political structure relative to the enactment of law and the control of administration. Every system of democratic government will exalt the people's representatives to a position of absolute sovereignty.
4. The field of politics sets the task for administration but

the field of administration lies outside the proper sphere of politics.

5. All modern governments will have a strong structural similarity so far as administrative functions are concerned.

6. Perfection in the hierarchical ordering of a professionally trained public service provides the structural conditions necessary for "good" administration.

7. Perfection in hierarchical organization will maximize efficiency as measured by least cost expended in money and effort.

8. Perfection of "good" administration as above defined is a necessary condition for modernity in human civilization and for the advancement of human welfare.

If these basic propositions advanced by Wilson are representative of a paradigm used in constituting a scholarly tradition, we would expect other scholars to present similar theoretical formulations. We would also expect research efforts to be predicated upon these same theoretical foundations. To indicate the generality of the paradigm, I shall briefly consider the congruence of Wilson's paradigm with Max Weber's theory of bureaucracy,[4] and with the governmental research and administrative survey tradition.

Weber's Theory of Bureaucracy

CONGRUENCE

Max Weber was concerned with the development of a general social theory which would provide an understanding of human civilization. Bureaucracy, for Weber, was a necessary condition, or an organizational means, for maintaining the legal, economic, and technical rationality inherent in modern civilization. Weber viewed the modern state as being "monocratic" or single-centered. (Gerth and Mills, 1946:214; Rheinstein, 1954:349-350.)[5] Rationality in administration depended upon a structure

[29]

of hierarchical relationships. Weber's work sustains all of Wilson's essential theses. The congruence in their work is immediately revealed in a brief synopsis of some of Weber's key points of emphasis.

Bureaucratic organizations, for Weber, are technically superior to all other forms of organization—comparable to the technical superiority of a machine over non-mechanical modes of production. Precision, speed, knowledge, continuity, discretion, unity, strict subordination, reduction of friction and of material and personal costs are the attributes of strictly bureaucratic administration. (Gerth and Mills, 1946:214.) Bureaucracy emphasizes an "objective" organization of conduct according to calculable rules without regard to persons. (Gerth and Mills, 1946:215.) A bureaucratic official conducts his office with formalistic impersonality applying the rule to the factual situation without hatred or passion. "Bureaucracy has a 'rational' character: rules, means, ends, and matter-of-factness dominate its bearings." (Gerth and Mills, 1946:244.)

Weber concurs with Wilson's position that perfection in bureaucratic administration depends upon rigorous exclusion of politics from the routines of administration. Bureaucracy depends upon the technical application of calculable rules of law to factual situations in a logically rigorous and machine-like manner. This rational character of bureaucratic administration led Weber, like Wilson, to associate bureaucratization with the development of modern civilization. "The nature of modern civilization, especially its technical-economic substructure," according to Weber, requires the "calculability of consequences" realized by bureaucratic organization. (Rheinstein, 1954:350.)

Above all, bureaucratization offers the optimal possibility for the realization of the principle of division of labor in administration according to purely technical considerations, allocating individual tasks to functionaries who are trained as specialists and who continuously add to their experiences by constant practice. (Rheinstein, 1954:350.)

The advance of modern civilization and the perfection of bureaucracy, presumably, go hand in hand.

ANOMALIES

Max Weber's characterization of bureaucracy is largely associated with his specification of the *conditions* of bureaucratic organization as an ideal type. When Weber goes on to consider the social and political consequences associated with the *perfection* of bureaucratic organization, he presents some highly anomalous themes.[6] "Where the bureaucratization of administration has been completely carried through," Weber anticipates that "a form of power relationship is established which is virtually indestructible." (Gerth and Mills, 1946:228.) It is an instrument that can be "easily made to work for anybody who knows how to gain control over it." (Gerth and Mills, 1946:228.) Bureaucracy, in effect, will serve any political master. "Hence," according to Weber, "the bureaucratic machinery continues to function for the successful revolutionaries or the occupying enemy just as it has been functioning for the legal government." (Rheinstein, 1954:xxxiv.)

When viewed from the perspectives of the individual bureaucrat, the virtual indestructibility of the perfected bureaucratic machine implies, in Weber's words, that:

The individual bureaucrat cannot squirm out of the apparatus in which he is harnessed. [T]he professional bureaucrat is chained to his activity by his entire material and ideal existence. [H]e is only a single cog in an ever moving mechanism which prescribes for him an essentially fixed route of march.... The individual bureaucrat is thus

[31]

forged to the community of all the functionaries who are integrated into the mechanism. (Gerth and Mills, 1946:228.)

The ruled are as powerless as the individual bureaucrat in dealing with the fully developed bureaucratic apparatus. Once perfected, the bureaucratic apparatus cannot, according to Weber, be dispensed with or be replaced. "If the official stops working, or if his work is forcefully interrupted, chaos results and it is difficult to improvise replacements from among the governed who are fit to master such chaos." (Gerth and Mills, 1946:229.) More and more the material fate of the masses depends upon the operation of bureaucratic organizations. "The idea of eliminating these organizations," Weber concludes, "becomes more and more utopian." (Gerth and Mills, 1946:229.)

In the context of these observations, Weber notes that altering the course of conduct in a bureaucratic machine normally depends upon the initiative of those at the very top. However, he goes on to indicate the powerlessness of those at the top:

> Under normal conditions, the power position of a fully developed bureaucracy is always overtowering. The 'political master' finds himself in the position of the 'dilettante' who stands opposite the 'expert,' facing the trained official who stands within the management of administration. (Gerth and Mills, 1946:232.)

Weber contends that this powerlessness of the "master" holds whether the master is a "people," a "parliament," an "aristocracy," a "popularly elected president" or a "monarch." (Gerth and Mills, 1946: 232–233). "The absolute monarch is powerless opposite the superior knowledge of the bureaucratic expert. . . ." (Gerth and Mills, 1946:234.) Weber also anticipates a coalition of interest between the head of government and the bureaucratic apparatus as against desires of party chiefs operating within legislative bodies in a constitutional government. (Gerth and Mills, 1946:234.)

From this portrait of a "fully developed bureaucracy" we can only conclude that the bureaucratic machine will place the professional bureaucrat in chains, will transform citizens into dependent masses and will make impotent "dilettantes" of their political "masters." The dominance of a fully developed bureaucracy would render all forms of constitutional rule equally irrelevant. Bureaucracy becomes the exclusive political reality. So far as I know, Weber never attempted to resolve the anomaly or paradox implied by the conclusions he reached about the "full" development of his "ideal" form.[7] He does, however, indicate that the dominance of a bureaucracy depends upon its capacity to monopolize information behind a facade of secrecy, to preclude competitive rivalry among aspiring officials, and to monopolize the professional expertise available in a society. (Gerth and Mills, 1946: 233–235.)

The Research Tradition
in American Public Administration

American scholarship in public administration, with a few exceptions, has had little concern for the picture that Max Weber portrayed of the fully developed bureaucracy.[8] Much of the research in American public administration has made little use of the predictive value of theory to derive hypotheses from theory and then using evidence to support or reject the hypotheses as a test of theory. American public administration is more preoccupied with theory as prescriptive doctrine which can be used to rationalize and reorganize the structure of administrative relations in accordance with the principles of hierarchical organization. The principles are taken as eternal truths which can "rescue executive methods from the confusion and costliness of empirical experiment...." (Wilson, 1887:210.)

Research in the mainstream of American public administration is usually undertaken with explicit reference to some agency or unit of government. The agency or government jurisdiction, thus, becomes the unit of analysis. The precepts of the Wilsonian paradigm provide a conceptual yardstick to assess patterns of organization that do not measure up to those precepts. Recommended policy changes are usually made to bring organizational arrangements into conformance with those precepts. Where a unit of government exercises general authority over the provision of numerous public services, the standard format of administrative surveys includes a diagnostic assessment of pathologies attributed to the proliferation of agencies, the fragmentation of authority, overlapping jurisdictions, and duplication of services. Duplication of services and overlapping jurisdictions are presumed, on *prima facie* grounds, to be wasteful and inefficient. The proliferation of agencies and fragmentation of authority are presumed to provoke conflict, and create disorder and deadlock.

Where research in this tradition focuses upon a community of people which is not organized as a unit of government, as in the case of a metropolitan region or a river basin, the axiomatics are simply pushed back a step. In such a case, any community of people must be constituted into a single unit of government with a single center of authority culminating in a unified command. A professionally trained public service organized into a chain of command responsible to a single chief executive will efficiently and responsibly discharge public policies in providing for the overall needs of the community.

Building upon the basic precepts in the Wilsonian paradigm, students of public administration gradually articulated several principles of administration. Such concepts as unity of command, span of control, chain of command, departmentalization by major functions, and direction by single heads of authority in subordinate units of administration are assumed to have universal applicability in the perfection of administrative arrangements. Strengthening of the government is viewed as the equivalent of increasing the authority and powers of the chief executive. General-authority agencies are preferred to limited-authority agencies. Large jurisdictions are preferred to small. Centralized solutions are preferred to the disaggregation of authority among diverse decision structures.[9]

The culmination of this research tradition is often identified with the work of the President's Commitee on Administrative Management. The President's Committee indeed affirms the essential theses in Wilson's theory of administration. Efficiency in government, according to the Committee's *Report,* depends upon two conditions: 1) the consent of the governed, and 2) good management. The first condition is assured according to the Committee's *Report* by the democratic character of the American Constitution.[10] The second condition, efficient management, however, "must be built into the structure of government just as it is built into a piece of machinery." (U.S. President's Committee, 1937:3.) The principles of efficient management "have emerged universally wherever men have worked together for some common purpose, whether through the state, the church, the private association, or the commercial enterprise." (U.S. President's Committee, 1937:3.) The Committee implied that principles of efficient management apply to all *associations* alike. The principles of management, summarized as "canons of efficiency," were assumed to require "the establishment of a responsible and effective chief executive as the center

[35]

of energy, direction, and administrative management; the systematic organization of all activity in the hands of a qualified personnel under the direction of the chief executive; and to aid him in this, the establishment of appropriate managerial and staff agencies." (U.S. President's Committee, 1937:3.)

Similarity between the "canons of efficiency" and the traditional principles of hierarchical organization, however, conceals a basic discontinuity in the theory of organization used by the President's Committee in conceptualizing its work. This discontinuity was expressed best by Luther Gulick, a member of the President's Committee and the author of a memorandum on the theory of organization prepared for the Committee's use and for the guidance of its staff. That memorandum is often identified as a classical restatement of the traditional theory of public administration. Luther Gulick's "Notes on the Theory of Organization," however, represent an anomalous orthodoxy which deserves careful scrutiny. (Gulick and Urwick, 1937: 3–45.) While sustaining an argument on behalf of a general theory of organization, Gulick advances theses which challenge the very foundations of the traditional theory of public administration.

Gulick's Anomalous Orthodoxy

Gulick's essay on the theory of organization begins with a traditional statement of the problem of organization as arising from a need to coordinate work subject to a high degree of specialization and division of labor. Such coordination is attained through "a structure of authority [which] requires not only many men at work in many places at selected times, but also a single directing executive authority." (Gulick and Urwick, 1937:7.) The concept of unity of command, the notion that "one man cannot serve two masters" is central to Gulick's theory of organization. (Gulick and Urwick, 1937:9.) It is the function

[36]

of organization to enable a director to coordinate and energize all of the subdivisions of work so that the major objective or task may be achieved efficiently.

PRINCIPLE OF HOMOGENEITY

Following this introduction to his analysis, Gulick presents a concept which he identifies as the principle of homogeneity. The principle of homogeneity implies that the means must be instrumental to the accomplishment of a particular task. Associating two or more non-homogeneous functions would sacrifice technical efficiency in administration by mixing factors of production which would have the effect of obstructing or impairing the net social product. An educational program, for example, might be impaired if combined with a law enforcement program. Public welfare administration should, similarly, be separated from police administration. "No one," Gulick contends, "would think of combining water supply and public education, or tax administration and public recreation." (Gulick and Urwick, 1937:10.) Those functions are too heterogeneous to be combined in a single agency. Gulick also contends that "politics" and "administration" are heterogeneous functions which cannot be combined within the structure of administration without producing inefficiency. (Gulick and Urwick, 1937:10.)

If there are limits upon the grouping of agencies which would impair technical efficiency, then the central precepts in Wilson's theory of administration come tumbling down. Efficiency in administration measured in the accomplishment of work at least cost is not necessarily attained through perfection in hierarchical organization. There may be circumstances where hierarchical organization will violate the principle of homogeneity and impair administrative efficiency.

Gulick discussed the difficulty of attaining a hierarchical ordering among the municipal agencies of the City of New York under these circumstances. The Charter Commission of 1934 reached the conclusion that municipal agencies could not be grouped into fewer than 25 departments without a loss of efficiency from the grouping of heterogeneous functions. A solution was attained by reorganizing the mayor's office to include three or four assistant mayors. Gulick concluded that this arrangement solved the problem inherent in the conflict between the principles of span of control and of homogeneity "provided the assistant mayors keep out of the technology of the services and devote themselves to the broad aspects of administration and coordination as would the mayor himself." (Gulick and Urwick, 1937:12.) Gulick, thus, turns to the organization of the executive—meaning the exercise of management activities associated with "the job of the chief executive" (Gulick and Urwick, 1937:13)— to solve the problems of executive control over agencies performing many heterogeneous functions.

Gulick invented the famous acronym POSDCORB to characterize *the work of the chief executive.* The acronym, as every student of public administration knows, stands for the following activities: planning, organizing, staffing, directing, coordinating, reporting and budgeting. Gulick notes that several of these functions were being separately institutionalized through different agencies of the Federal government. Budgeting was organized through the Bureau of the Budget; planning through the National Resources Committee; and staffing through the Civil Service Commission. Each of these agencies was viewed by Gulick as "a managerial arm of the chief executive." (Gulick and Urwick, 1937:14.) Together these agencies might be organized as part of a managerial establishment in the Executive Offices of the President.

The Jungle Gym

Having introduced a series of management functions which he associated with *the work of the chief executive,* Gulick then analyses the task of organizing the "work" units of government without violating the principle of homogeneity. He suggests that each activity can be classified in accordance with the major *purpose* being served, the *process* being utilized, the *persons or clientele* being served, and the *place* where the service is being rendered. He then suggests that each of these categories can be used as a basis for constituting work units and that one need not be exclusive of another. He, thus, speaks of vertical and horizontal departments by indicating that a particular department can be organized vertically to serve a major *purpose* such as the provision of public health services. Such activities may also have reference to *processes* requiring such diverse specialties as medicine, law, accounting, engineering, personnel services which can be organized into horizontal departments. The principle of "a single structure of authority" had somehow dissolved into a "fabric of organizational interrelations" with multiple networks of cross-departmentalization. (Gulick and Urwick, 1937: Chart III, 19.) The symmetry of a hierarchical pyramid was abandoned for the lattice-work of a "jungle gym." (Gulick and Urwick, 1937:20.)

Whether to rely primarily upon one or another mode of organization in constituting departments or work units is a matter of calculating the relative advantages and disadvantages of each. Whichever mode is used as a primary basis of organization does not exclude the possibility of developing secondary, tertiary or quarternary networks of organization to gain some of the residual advantage afforded by the other methods of organization. "In an organization built on two or more bases of departmentalization," Gulick suggests, "the executive may use the process departments as a routine means of coordinating the purpose departments." (Gulick and Urwick, 1937:34.) One chain of command can, in effect, be used as a tool for coordinating alternate structures of command.

THE HOLDING COMPANY IDEA

Gulick then introduces "The Holding Company Idea" to suggest that:

> a large enterprise engaged in many complicated activities which do not require extensive or intimate coordination may need only the loosest type of central coordinating authority. Under such conditions, each activity may be set up, on a purpose basis, as virtually independent, and the central structure of authority may be nothing more than a holding company. (Gulick and Urwick, 1937:34.)

The central coordinating authority in such circumstances could relax the primary structure of control and sustain coordination through secondary or tertiary organizations.

By analogy each department of government is likened unto a subsidiary. The President is chief executive of the holding company. The Executive Offices of the President became the embodiment of the holding company idea. The managerial agencies of the government which performed the POSDCORB functions would be integrated into the holding company structure. Each would operate as one of several management bureaus. Gulick anticipated that in such a circumstance each department "would be given extensive freedom to carry on as it saw fit and the President at the center of the parent company would not pretend to do more than prevent conflict and competition." (Gulick and Urwick, 1937:34.)

Gulick argued that *not* all the activities of government can be appropriately departmentalized on the basis of a single plan of organization. (Gulick and Urwick, 1937: 31–32.) Different bases of departmentalization can be used and the choice of which to use is calculated on the basis of relative advantage. The choice of one basis for the first order of departmentalization does not preclude the development of secondary or tertiary forms of organization. The organization of the executive can have recourse to multiple management processes and multiple control structures. A multiple command structure was clearly implied.

Yet, Gulick poses his problem in traditional terms and reaffirms conventional wisdom. He is not prepared to abandon the maxim that "a man cannot serve two masters." (Gulick and Urwick, 1937: 31-37.) The principle of unity of command presumably can be preserved if *everyone* serves but *one master*. The simple concept of hierarchy is replaced by a complex "fabric of organizational interrelationships" resembling a "jungle gym" but controlled by a single chief executive. (Gulick and Urwick, 1937:19-20.) The management apparatus inherent in the holding company concept with its managing bureaus exercising control over operational agencies necessarily means that the management of each operating agency confronts a multiple command structure. The head of each operating agency might eventually find himself in a position comparable to a sergeant receiving commands from a platoon of officers. Unity of command is preserved if the jungle gym apparatus of the Executive Offices can be penetrated to gain access to the President as "the center of energy, direction and administrative management." (U.S. President's Committee, 1937: 3.)

More than a half-century of intellectual effort in American study of public administration was predicated upon an assumption that perfection in the hierarchical organization of administrative arrangements is synonomous with efficiency. Luther Gulick introduced the principle of homogeneity to indicate limits upon efficiency in the aggregation of administrative operations into ever larger units of organization. Gulick's effort to provide an alternative structure led him to consider alternative ways for aggregating work units and to suggest the possibility of primary, secondary, tertiary, and quartenary networks of organization. The principle of unity of command was retained by reference to the holding company concept and Gulick returned from his speculative foray to reaffirm the conventional wisdom, that "a man cannot serve two masters." (Gulick and Urwick, 1937: 9.)

Simon's Challenge

Herbert Simon undertook the frontal attack which Gulick had avoided. Simon uses the criterion of efficiency as his basic tool to *define* what is meant by "good" or "correct" administration. "The criterion of efficiency," according to Simon, "dictates that choice which produces the largest result from the given application of resources." (Simon, 1947:179.) Where output is specified, the criterion of efficiency determines which alternative form of organization is best.

Using the criterion of efficiency, Simon makes a critical examination of the traditionally accepted principles of administration and demonstrates that those principles do not necessarily hold. Increases in specialization as such will not necessarily increase efficiency. Only those increases in specialization that improve performance when the available resources are given would lead to an increase in efficiency.

Similarly, Simon takes Gulick to task for his return

to the haven afforded by the principle of unity of command. A certain amount of "irresponsibility and confusion" might well ensue from relaxing the principle of unity of command, but Simon insists that such costs may not be "too great a price to pay" for the benefits to be derived from alternative modes of organization. (Simon, 1947:24.) If the benefits from relaxing the principle of unity of command exceeded the costs, then the efficiency of an organization would be improved as a consequence of such relaxation.

In his effort to reconstruct a theory of administration, Simon endeavors to develop a theory of rational choice. He insists upon a fact-value distinction in the sense that factual circumstances are concerned with the calculation of probable consequences and evaluation is concerned with the calculation of preferences. The task in decision making is to consider different strategic alternatives, to anticipate the probable consequences which would follow factually from those alternatives. Given a complete and consistent set of factual premises and a complete and consistent set of value premises, the criterion of efficiency would imply that there is only one alternative that is preferable to all other alternatives. (Simon, 1947:223.) Only one decision would in such circumstances be consistent with rationality. A theory of rational choice under conditions of perfect information and a transitively ordered schedule of preferences permits no choice. The correct solution is fully determinate.

The essential problem in administrative organization is that of enhancing rationality in human choice, given the radical limits inherent in the psychology of choice. (Simon, 1947:240-244.) Human capabilities for handling information, arraying preferences and acting in relation to appropriate alternatives are subject to severe limitations. Cooperative teamwork requires the exercise of discretion by each member of an organization. Coordina-

[43]

tion of each individual's actions depends upon the provision of appropriate factual premises and value premises so as to facilitate a rational choice in his exercise of discretion.

The function of organization is to bound the rationality exercised by each person as a decision maker working within an organization. The bounding of discretion by the specification of factual and value premises leads Simon, following Barnard's pioneering work on *The Functions of the Executive,* to conceptualize authority as being "zoned." (Simon, 1947: 123–153; Barnard, 1938: 168–169.) Presumably the specification of limits to areas of acceptance might derive from different sources of authority. An organization thus might reflect a composite of command networks rather than a single line of authority or chain of command.

The concepts of bounded rationality and zoned authority enable Simon to conceptualize an organization as being an equilibrium maintained within areas of acceptance established by the different constituent elements of an organization. He conceptualizes the constituent elements as "customers," "employees" and "entrepreneurs." (Simon, 1947:111 ff.) The entrepreneur reflects the control group in an organization; and the employment contract establishes the area of acceptance within which employees are willing to accept direction from management in guiding their actions. Customers in turn provide funds in exchange for products. These funds supply the incentives for the entrepreneur and the employees to function as a productive team or organization. Simon conceptualizes the legislature as being the equivalent of "customers" in supplying a public agency with its funds; but a legislature also functions as a control group. (Simon, 1947: 120–121.) Simon does not attempt to untangle the implications for organizational equilibrium when a legislature simultaneously attempts to articulate consumer preferences and to operate as a control group.

An equilibrium model of organization implies that the area of acceptance is derived by agreement among the persons involved in an organization. Basic issues which go beyond the areas of acceptance are subject to negotiation or to resolution by recourse to decision structures external to "the" organization. Simon's concept of organization as an equilibrium maintained within areas of acceptance has been used by James D. Thompson, for example, to express the concept of organization as a "domain consensus." (J.D. Thompson, 1967:28.) Administration becomes the management of interdependencies among the constituent elements within an organization in relation to opportunities and threats in a dynamic environment. (J.D. Thompson, 1967: 34-38.)

Within the context of a means-ends calculus inherent in purposive action, the problem of efficiency can be conceptualized as either minimizing the costs of production in relation to a particular output or of maximizing the output for a given level of expenditure. Simon explicitly recognizes the difficulty of establishing an explicit and measurable "social production function" when the service being rendered is the provision of police protection, the maintenances of public health, or some other public service. (Simon, 1947: 188-190.) In view of this difficulty, Simon reaches the conclusion that, "It is hard to see how rationality can play any significant role in the formulation of administrative decisions unless these production functions are at least approximately known." (Simon, 1947: 189.)

Simon's challenge to the Wilsonian tradition in the study of public administration was of radical proportions. The criterion of efficiency was used to reject the presumption that perfection in hierarchical organization is synonymous with efficiency. In pursuit of his analysis, he formulates a theory of rational choice which is a general theory that might be applied to any aspect of social organization. Yet, he curiously confines his analysis to something that he calls "an" organization or "the" organization.[11] The sets of events which Simon labels as an "organization" are uniformly characterized by a hierarchical ordering. While rejecting unity of command as being a logically necessary condition for efficiency in any and all circumstances, Simon repeatedly returns to face the fact of hierarchy in his discussion of administrative behavior.

Simon, in considering the function of social organization, recognizes that:

> Institutional arrangements are subject to infinite variations, and can hardly be said to follow from any innate characteristics of man. Since these institutions largely determine the mental sets of the participants they set the conditions for the exercise of... rationality in human society. (Simon, 1947:101.)

He then goes on to indicate that, "The highest level of integration that man can achieve consists in taking an existing set of institutions as one alternative and comparing it with other sets." (Simon, 1947:101.) He does *not,* however, apply this principle to the problem of administrative behavior by comparing one set of organizations with other sets of organizations to establish the relative efficiency of different organizational arrangements.

In considering institutional arrangements in a democratic society, Simon indicates that "legislation is the principal designer and arbiter of these institutions." (Simon, 1947:101.) But, what theory of institutions is to guide legislators in their choice of designs for conceptualizing and formulating the institutional setting that establish the basic premises for human rationality? By bounding his own theory of organization with a preoccupation for intra-organizational arrangements Simon reduced the theoretical impact of his challenge. By leaving legislatures in the position of being the principal designers and ultimate arbiters of institutional arrangements, the traditional dichotomy of politics and administration is sustained. The criterion of efficiency becomes a tool for suboptimization.[12] A theory of bounded rationality without the appropriate institutional constraints can become a theory of bounded irrationality.[13] Administrative behavior is bounded by institutional constraints other than those internal to "the organization." Public administration requires reference to more than the theory of a firm.

Simon challenged and his challenge stands. But having challenged, Simon returned to the world of bureaucratic organizations to pursue his work within the familiar constraints of a social universe dichotomized into the domains of politics and administration. Another community of scholars, concerned with conditions of institutional weakness and institutional failure in market economies, is pursuing similar interests in the study of non-market decision making. These scholars, many of whom are oblivious to the intellectual controversies in public administration, are fashioning a new theory of public choice and collective enterprise. We shall turn to their work in the next lecture.

The Work of the Contemporary Political Economists

Introduction

A PERSISTENT THEME IN THE INTELLECTUAL MAINSTREAM of American public administration is reference to efficiency as an essential criterion of "good" administration. Efficiency is conceptualized in two fundamentally different ways. One way views efficiency as being expressed through principles of hierarchical organization. The greater the degree of specialization, professionalization, and linear organization in a unitary chain of command, the greater the efficiency.[1] The other way views efficiency in terms of a cost calculus. The accomplishment of a specifiable objective at least cost; or, a higher level of performance at a given cost is the measure of efficiency. Wilson clearly assumed that perfection in hierarchical organization is equivalent to efficiency measured in a cost calculus. (Wilson, 1887:197. See also proposition 6, p. 29 *supra.*) Wilson, thus, equated perfection in hierarchical organization with least-cost performance.

Gulick, at the very culmination of the administrative survey movement, challenged Wilson's assumption by specifying a principle of homogeneity as a limit to efficiency in hierarchical organization. Simon sustained that challenge and explicitly broke with the traditional theory of administration. Using the least-cost solution as his criterion of efficiency, Simon demonstrated that solutions based upon perfection in hierarchical organization need not be the most efficient. Simon recognized that various institutional arrangements might be used to bound human rationality and affect the potential for attaining efficiency.

However, Simon chose to confine his works largely to something that might be specified as "an" organization or "the" organization. "Organizations" in this sense became the primary focus for subsequent work on organization theory. This focus led to substantial emphasis upon the problems of bounded rationality *within* an organization and to substantial neglect of different decision-making arrangements and of multi-organizational arrangements in administrative systems.

The challenge posed by Simon's work has been pursued by a community of scholars who use the criterion of efficiency to assess performance in the provision of public goods and services. Most of these scholars were trained as economists with specialized interests in agricultural economics, resource economics, public finance, public utilities, public regulations and welfare economics more generally. Since their analytical tools derive from economic theory and their concern is with public decision making, I shall identify this group of scholars as contemporary political economists.[2]

Many early efforts of these political economists were largely oriented toward benefit-cost analysis. One facet of this work has evolved into the Planning, Programming, and Budgeting System for planning public expenditure decisions. (U. S. Congress, 1969.) PPB analysis, however, rests upon theoretical presumptions similar to the traditional theory of public administration. Such analysts would find Leonard White's early definition of public administration as the *"management of men and materials in the accomplishment of the purposes of the state"* (White, 1939:66. White's emphasis.) as appropriate if the term "nation" were substituted for "state." The PPB analyst takes the methodological perspective of an "Omniscient Observer."[3] Assuming that he knows the "will of the state," the PPB analyst then selects a program for the efficient utilization of resources (i.e., men and material) in the accomplishment of those purposes. The assumption of omniscience may not hold; and, as a consequence, PPB may involve radical errors and generate gross inefficiencies. (Wildavsky, 1966.)

In the last ten to fifteen years, other political economists have turned their attention to the relationship of institutional arrangements to economic performance in the public sector. The presentation in this lecture will be confined to those political economists who 1) use the individual as the basic unit of analysis, 2) use the theory of externalities, common properties, and public goods to define the structure of events relevant to public administration, 3) analyze the consequences that different organizational or decision-making arrangements have upon the output of public goods or services, and 4) evaluate these consequences by whether or not the outcome is consistent with the efficiency criterion.

Model of Man

Work among most political economists is usually based upon an explicit model of man. They adopt a form of methodological individualism which makes self-conscious use of the perspective of a representative individual or set of representative individuals in the conduct of analysis. (Buchanan, 1966:26ff.) The representative individual may be a member of a hypothetical community, an entrepreneur, a public employee, or some other person

[50]

whose interests are explicitly stated. Assumptions about individuals normally include reference to 1) self-interest, 2) rationality, 3) information, 4) law and order, and 5) the choice of a maximizing strategy.

The assumption of self-interest implies primarily that each individual has preferences which affect the decisions which he makes; and those preferences may differ from individual to individual. Rationality is usually defined as the ability to rank all known alternatives available to the individual in a consistent manner. (Downs, 1957:4-6.) Assumptions about information usually have reference to three levels of information which are defined as certainty, risk, and uncertainty. (Knight, 1921.) Under either certainty or risk, an analyst can project a relatively determinant solution to a particular problem. Under conditions of uncertainty, the determinateness of solutions is replaced by conclusions about the *range* of possible solutions.

Once uncertainty is postulated, a further assumption may be made that an individual *learns* about states of affairs as he develops and tests strategies. (Simon, 1959.) Estimates are made about the consequences of strategies. If the predictions follow, then a more reliable image of the world is established. If predicted events fail to occur, an individual is forced to change his image of the world and modify his strategies. (Shackle, 1961.) Where learning occurs, the assumption of rationality may also have to be modified to allow for a reordering of preferences as the individual learns more about the opportunity costs inherent in different alternatives.

An assumption of uncertainty also implies that one of the essential considerations in the design of organizational arrangements is the development and use of information. (Cyert and March, 1963.) Planning and deliberation are activities that seek to clarify alternatives and the consequences that are likely to flow from those alter-

[51]

natives. An essential criterion of organizational arrangements is the extent to which relevant information is evoked or excluded and the effect that such organizational characteristics have upon the error-proneness or error-correcting propensities of decision makers.

Classical economic theory postulates that economic man will act within the limits of "lawful" conduct. Most analysis by political economists is predicated upon some postulated condition of law and order where basic definitions of rights, duties, privileges, and exposures exist in some form. An assumption may either be made that some basic constitutional settlement exists in the larger political environment or among segments of the domain being considered. In short, some political structure is assumed as providing a context for analysis. In the absence of any law and order assumption, it might be necessary to assume a Hobbesian state of war as the prevailing human condition.

The assumption that individuals will adopt a maximizing strategy implies the consistent choice of those alternatives which an individual thinks will provide the greatest net benefit as weighed by his own preferences. This can be expressed alternatively as the choice of the least-cost strategy and is equivalent to the efficiency criterion. Maximization under uncertainty is not possible in a formal mathematical sense. Yet, it is possible to assume that individuals will attempt to maximize subject to uncertainty. In that case, an individual who pursues a maximizing strategy in the absence of knowledge of all alternatives and of the costs of learning about added possibilities would act *as if* he were "satisficing." (March and Simon, 1958: 140–141.)

Structure of Events

Political economists assume that rational, self-interested individuals who pursue maximizing strategies will face a variety of situations.[4] The structure of events inherent in different situations can be characterized by their relative divisibility or indivisibility. The degree to which events can be subject to *control* by individual persons through *possession, exchange,* or *use* is the critical criterion in establishing their divisibility or indivisibility. Those events which cannot be subject to possession, exchange, or use by individuals have the characteristics of involving interdependencies and commonalities in their possession and/or use.

Events involved in any decision-making situation can be arrayed on a continuum ranging from purely private to purely public. (Davis and Whinston, 1967.) Goods are events for which people have preferences; bads are events for which people have aversions. The potential demand for most goods will exceed supply; and goods will be scarce. The supply of most bads will exceed demands and thus require efforts to restrict or alter their supply. *Purely private goods* are defined as those which are highly divisible and can be packaged, contained, or measured in discrete units. Purely private goods are subject to provision under competitive market conditions where potential consumers can be *excluded* from enjoying the benefit unless they are willing to pay the price. *Purely public goods,* by contrast, are highly indivisible. Potential consumers *cannot* be easily excluded from enjoying the benefit once a public good is produced. Once public goods are provided for some, they are available for others to enjoy without reference to who pays the costs. (Samuelson, 1954:387; Margolis, 1955.) National defense is a classic example of such a good. Once it is provided for some individuals living within a nation, it is automatically provided for all individuals within the nation whether they pay for it or not.

In addition to the two logical categories of purely public and purely private goods, most political economists would postulate the existences of an intermediate continuum. (Mishan, 1969.) Within this continuum, the production or consumption of goods or services may involve *spillover effects* or *externalities* which are not isolated and contained within market transactions. (Ayres and Kneese, 1969.) Goods with appreciable externalities are similar to private goods to the extent that some effects can be subject to the exclusion principle. However, other effects are like public goods and impinge upon persons not directly involved. Water pollution is an example of a negative externality; the benefits which other members of a community derive from a person acquiring an education would be a positive externality. A reduction in the cost of a negative externality and an increase in the yield of positive externalities are both equivalent to the provision of a public good.

Common-property resources have attributes somewhat analogous to public goods. (Gordon, 1954; Christy and Scott, 1965:ch. 2.) Common-property resources involve a jointness of supply and a separability of use where individuals cannot be effectively excluded from access to the supply of a resource but each individual makes a separable use of that resource. A ground water basin, for example, affords a common water supply which is accessible to any overlying property owner. Once extracted, the water becomes available for the separable use of each overlying proprietor. Whenever the aggregate demand upon such a resource exceeds the available supply, one person's increased demand will adversely affect the use of others. Beyond certain thresholds of supply, an exclusion principle will operate among users so that one person's use will impair use by others, but the supply of the resource continues to be subject to a high degree of interdependency and indivisibility. Spillover effects occur in relation to conditions of supply and may or may not occur in relation to conditions of use.

[54]

The work of political economists is based upon an assumption that self-interested individuals, who pursue maximizing strategies, will require reference to appropriate sets of decision rules or decision-making arrangements in dealing with different structures of events if the welfare potential of a community of individuals is to be enhanced. No single form of organization is presumed to be "good" for all circumstances.[5] Rather, any one type of organizational arrangement can generate a limited range of preferred effects. Every organizational arrangement will be subject to limitations. Institutional weaknesses and institutional failures will become apparent if those limits are exceeded. Thus, any particular type of organizational arrangement will have certain capabilities and will be subject to sources of weakness or failure. The essential problem in the theory of organization is to 1) anticipate the consequences which follow when 2) self-interested individuals choose maximizing strategies within 3) particular organizational arrangements when applied to 4) particular structures of events. The optimum choice of organizational arrangements would be that which minimizes the costs associated with institutional weakness or institutional failure. (Buchanan, 1969.)

The type of analysis made by political economists in assessing the consequences that decision rules have upon the choice of strategy in different situations will be applied to four different decision-making arrangements. The first application will examine the effect of decision rules allowing for individualistic choice related to a common-property or public-good situation. The second application will examine the effect of decision rules characteristic of large-scale bureaucratic organizations concerned with the provision of public goods and services.

Given the problem of institutional weakness and institutional failure associated both with individualistic choice and with large-scale bureaucratic establishments, consideration will then be given to the choice of decision rules that would enable a community of people to reduce these costs by organizing a collective enterprise to develop a common-property resource or provide a public good. Finally, consideration will be given to the development of multi-organizational arrangements as a means of providing for a heterogeneous mix of diverse public goods and services.

INDIVIDUALISTIC CHOICE AND THE TRAGEDY OF THE COMMONS

Individualistic choice occurs whenever each person is free to decide for himself in the pursuit of his own interest. Individualistic choice is characteristic of the market and occurs whenever the only requirement is the willing consent of those individuals who freely agree or contract with one another to exchange some good or undertake some action. If each person is free to decide for himself in the pursuit of his own interest where a common-property resource or a public good is involved, some serious problems will occur. Each individual will maximize his own net welfare if he takes advantage of the common property or public good at minimum cost to himself. In the case of a public good, the cost minimizer would have no incentive to pay his share of the costs for provision. Most public goods would not be provided if funds were collected strictly on a voluntary basis.

In the case of a common-property resource with a renewable yield or supply, like that of a common water supply, individualistic choice has great advantages in reducing the costs of entrepreneurship so long as supply exceeds demands. However, when the aggregate demand of all individual users exceeds the available supply of a common-property resource, an increase in demand will diminish supplies and increase costs for the community of users. Each person will calculate only his own individual cost and will ignore the social costs imposed upon others. Many individuals will choose a "dog-in-the-manger" strategy, pursue their own advantage, and disregard the consequences for others. Furthermore, some individuals will be motivated to conceal information about their intentions. Should others propose joint action, those who conceal information may remain free to take advantage of opportunities created by the joint actions of others. If voluntary actions were taken to curtail demand, some individuals will pursue a "hold-out" strategy. (Hirshleifer, DeHaven, and Milliman, 1960.) The "hold-out" will be free to capture a lion's share of the benefits derived from the voluntary joint actions of his neighbors. As long as each person is free to decide his own course of action, the probability of someone pursuing a hold-out strategy is high. The presence of hold-outs will threaten the stability of any joint voluntary solution. (V. Ostrom, 1968.)

If the competitive dynamic is allowed to run its course, social costs will escalate to a point where continued operations will yield an economic loss for the community of users. Individuals in weak economic positions will be forced out. The neighborhood effects which are generated may include poverty, deprivations, threats, and even violence. Individualistic decision making applied to common-property resources will lead inexorably to tragedy unless the common property can be partitioned into separable private properties or decision-making arrangements can be modified to enable persons to act jointly in relation to a common property. This eventuality has been characterized by Garret Hardin as "the tragedy of the commons." (Hardin, 1968.) Unrestricted individualistic choice in relation to common-property resources or public goods can generate destructive competition where the greater the individual effort, the worse off people become.[6]

Because of this competitive dynamic, individuals cannot be expected to form *large voluntary* associations to pursue matters of common or public interest unless special conditions can be met. (Olson, 1965.) These conditions will exist only 1) when members can derive a separable benefit of a sufficient magnitude to cover the cost of membership, or 2) where they can be coerced through some form of levy or taxation into bearing their share of the costs. Thus, we cannot expect people to organize themselves voluntarily to secure the development of a common property or the provision of a public good.

When individuals act with the legal independence characteristic of decision making in market structures in a situation dominated by externalities, common-property resources, or public goods, we can conclude that *institutional weakness* or *institutional failure* will occur. The magnitude of the weakness or failure will depend upon the importance of the externality, or the degree of indivisibility occurring in the common property or public good.

BUREAUCRATIC ORGANIZATION

Bureaucratic organization is an alternative decision-making arrangement to that of individualistic choice. Bureaucratic organization implies reliance upon hierarchy where subordinates are required to defer to the commands of superiors in the selection of appropriate actions and are subject to sanctions or discipline for failure to do so. Bureaucratic organization can reduce some of the costs associated with the use of individualistic choice. The exercise of governmental prerogative by public officials capable of central direction and control implies that effective sanctions can be mobilized to preclude the hold-out strategy and to undertake management programs to develop a common property resource or produce a public good.

In the organization of any management program, recourse to a hierarchical command structure will permit economic advantage to be realized whenever production processes require a pooling of efforts through a division of labor which takes advantage of common production facilities. This rationale applies to both private firms and public agencies. If a firm can conduct business under the management of an entrepreneur at a lesser cost than if each and every transaction were organized as a market transaction, both the entrepreneur and the employees of the firm can derive a benefit from agreeing to act in accordance with the decisions of the entrepreneur in allocating work assignments among several different employees. (Coase, 1937.) Bureaucratic organization is a method for enhancing efficiency in operations by minimizing decision or transaction costs within the limits or zones of authority provided by the employment contract and the competitive force of the product market.

When principles of bureaucratic organization are applied to the conditions prevailing in the provision of public goods and services, a number of sources for potential institutional weakness or institutional failure become apparent. In the absence of an exclusion principle, the competitive force of a product market will not exist for most public organizations. (Downs, 1967: 29–30.) As a consequence entrepreneurs in such organizations will be less sensitive to diseconomies of scale which accrue from increasing management costs as the size of a public organization increases. We can anticipate that any organization might reach a point where the management cost of supervising an additional employee will exceed the marginal value added by the employee's productivity.

Beyond that point, a growth in organizational size will generate a net economic loss or yield a decreasing social return.

Gordon Tullock in *The Politics of Bureaucracy* (1965) analyzes the consequences which follow when rational, self-interested individuals pursue maximizing strategies in very large public bureaucracies. Tullock's "economic man" is an ambitious public employee who seeks to advance his career opportunities for promotions within a bureaucracy. Since career advancement depends upon favorable recommendations by his superiors, a career-oriented public servant will act so as to please his superiors. Favorable information will be forwarded; unfavorable information will be repressed. Distortion of information will diminish control and create expectations which diverge from events generated by actions. Large-scale bureaucracies will thus become error-prone and cumbersome in adapting to rapidly changing conditions. Efforts to correct the malfunctioning of bureaucracy by tightening control will simply magnify errors. A decline in return to scale can be expected to result. The larger the organization becomes, the smaller the percent of its activities will relate to output and the larger the proportion of its efforts will be expended on management.

Tullock suggests that the limits upon control in very large public bureaucracies will engender "bureaucratic free enterprise" (Tullock, 1965:167) where individuals and groups within an organization proceed with the formulation of their own missions with opportunities for side payoffs including graft and corruption. Goal displacement and risk avoidance motivated by individual self-interest will generate organizational dysfunctions as elaborate justifications are fabricated to cover potential exposures to the scrutiny of superior authorities. The social consequences generated by an organization become increasingly contradictory and unreal to an independent observer when compared to public rhetoric about organizational purposes and goals. Michel Crozier concluded his study of French bureaucracy by asserting that *"a bureaucratic organization is an organization that cannot correct its behavior by learning from its errors."* (Crozier, 1964:187. Crozier's emphasis.) Both Tullock and Crozier sustain an analysis of conditions giving rise to institutional weakness and failure in large bureaucratic organizations. Their analysis is fully consistent with Max Weber's portrait of the fully developed bureaucracy.[7]

Once a public good is provided, the absence of an exclusion principle also implies that each individual using such a good or service will have little choice but to take advantage of whatever is provided unless he is either able to move to another jurisdiction or wealthy enough to make separate provision for himself. (Tiebout, 1956.) Under these conditions, the producer of a public good may also be relatively free to induce savings in production costs by shifting some of the burdens or costs of production to users or consumers of the service. (Weschler and Warren, 1970.) Shifts of producer costs to users may result in an aggregate loss of efficiency if savings on the production side are exceeded by added costs on the consumption side. Public agencies rarely if ever, for example, calculate the value of a user's time and inconvenience when studies are made of how to make better use of an employee's time. More efficient use of clerical time may be more than off-set in the time spent by persons who stand in line waiting upon their "public servants." A net loss in efficiency may occur. (Weschler and Warren, 1970.) If a citizen has no place else to go, and if he is one in a multitude of other citizens, the probability of his interest being taken into account is negligible. The most impoverished members of a community are most exposed to deprivations under these circumstances. From this theoretical perspective, an analyst would not be surprised to find a positive relationship between the professionalization of the public service and the impoverishment of ghettos within big cities.

The inability of users of public goods and services to sustain an arm's length relationship with producers of public goods and services generates further problems when user preferences are subject to change in relation to the available supply of public goods and services. (E. Ostrom, 1971.) *No one* can know the preferences or values of other persons apart from giving them opportunities to express their preferences or values. If public agencies are organized in a way that does not allow for the expression of a diversity of preferences among different communities of people, then producers of public goods and services will be taking action without information as to the changing preferences of the persons they serve.[8] Expenditures will be made with little reference to consumer utility. *Producer efficiency in the absence of consumer utility is without economic meaning.*

Similar difficulties are engendered when conditions of demand for a public good or service increase in relation to the available supply. When demands begin to exceed supply, the dynamics inherent in "the tragedy of the commons" may arise all over again. A congested street or highway will, for example, carry less and less traffic as the demand grows. What was once a public "good" may now become a public "bad" as congested and noisy traffic precludes a growing number of opportunities for alternative uses. In short, public goods may be subject to serious *erosion* or *degradation* under conditions of changing demands. In the absence of a capability to respond with modified supply schedules and regulations for use, a public "good" may come to be a public "bad" and "the tragedy of the commons" can reach critical or explosive proportions. (Buchanan, 1970.)

The capacity to levy taxes, to make appropriate expenditure decisions and to provide the necessary public facilities is insufficient for optimality in the use of such facilities.[9] One pattern of use may impair the value of a common facility or a public good for another pattern of use. The development of water resource facilities, for example, will be insufficient to enhance welfare for members of a community of users without attention to basic rules and regulations controlling the use of such facilities by different sets of users. Use of streams for the discharge of waste can, for example, become a dominant use which will force out other users.

Optimal use of public facilities, when each use is not fully compatible with each other use, requires the development of a system of rules and regulations establishing capabilities and limitations in the discretion which persons can exercise in using common facilities made available to them. The development of such rules and regulations is relevant both to the scheduling of production processes and to the ordering of use patterns by potential users and consumers. These rules and regulations, like any set of decision rules, are not *self-generating, self-modifying, or self-enforcing.* Thus, we are confronted with the basic problems of *who* shall promulgate and enforce rules of conduct to govern relations among individuals who use common properties or public facilities in relation to what sets of interests. Administrative rules and regulations are, thus, *not* a matter of political indifference to the users of public goods and services.[10]

While bureaucratic organization will contribute significant institutional capabilities in the organization of any enterprise or agency concerned with the control of externalities, the management of a common property, or the provision of a public good, such a form of organization is also subject to serious conditions of institutional weakness and institutional failure. An optimal structure for a public enterprise will need to take account of diversities in user preferences and in production economies, relationship of demand to conditions of supply, and relationships where one pattern of use may impair other patterns of use. The very large bureaucracy will 1) become increasingly indiscriminating in its response to diverse demands, 2) impose increasingly high social costs upon those who are presumed to be the beneficiaries, 3) fail to proportion supply to demand, 4) allow public goods to erode by failing to take actions to prevent one use from impairing other uses, 5) become increasingly error prone and uncontrollable to the point where public actions deviate radically from rhetoric about public purposes and objectives, and 6) eventually lead to a circumstance where remedial actions exacerbate rather than ameliorate problems. The circumstances which generate institutional weakness and institutional failure in large-scale bureaucracies pose problems which require a reconsideration of the decision rules applicable to public enterprises.

THE CONSTITUTION OF SELF-GOVERNING PUBLIC ENTERPRISES

If individuals are to surmount the problems inherent in the tragedy of the commons and are to avoid the pathologies of the fully developed bureaucracy, they are confronted with the task of conceptualizing alternative institutional arrangements for the organization of collective or public enterprises. The structure of events inherent in a common-property resource or a public-good situation provides us with a basis for conceptualizing the community of interests which need to be taken into account in designing alternative institutional arrangements. An inchoate community is formed by the individuals who use or enjoy a common-property resource, or a public good.

The domain of the common property or the public good defines and bounds the community of interest.

If the object of interest can be identified, then courses of action can be examined to determine which alternatives will enhance the welfare of that community of individuals. If some form of joint action is available which would leave each individual better off provided that all members of the community were required to contribute proportionately to that activity, then each person will be motivated to devise and agree to a set of decision rules authorizing action on behalf of that community of individuals. Such rules would require some form of coercion to insure that each individual will discharge his proportionate share of the burden.

"Bureaucratic free enterprise" need not be the vice that Tullock implied if 1) a bureaucracy is immediately accountable to the relevant community of interest for whom it is acting, 2) the costs of providing a joint good are funded by the constituents in proportion to their benefit or in accordance with some comparable rule of equity, and 3) public facilities are subject to use under terms and conditions which are considered by the relevant community to be reasonably designed to advance their common welfare. If these conditions can be met, we can then contemplate the possibility of organizing a self-governing collective enterprise where the organizational structure is capable of internalizing decision-making arrangements appropriate to the community of interests associated with the management of a common property or the provision of a public good. Reliance upon external decision structures would be necessary only under conditions 1) where adequate remedies are not available for resolving local conflicts within the decision structures afforded by the constitution of such an enterprise, or 2) where the operation of a public enterprise is conducted in a manner that causes injuries to others outside its boundaries. If such conditions are to be met, *the structure of public administration cannot be organized apart from processes of political choice* which provide means for 1) the expression of social preferences of individuals within the community being served, 2) the formulation, enforcement, and revision of the decision rules governing both producer performance and conditions of consumer use, and 3) the articulation and enforcement of demands made by individual users as against the producers of public services.

In the production and exchange of purely private goods and services, money is a medium of exchange and can be used as a measure of value and as an expression of consumer utility. Public goods are not subject to exchange, and market price cannot be used as an appropriate measure of user preference. The constitution of public enterprises must depend instead upon the development of political mechanisms such as voting, representation, legislation, and adjudication for people to express their interests by signalling agreements or disagreements as the basis for ordering their relationships with one another. Such mechanisms provide essential means for informing public entrepreneurs about their strategic opportunities and limitations.

The development of organizational arrangements, which provides opportunities for persons to signal their agreements and disagreements, can be conceptualized as a problem of constitutional choice. (Buchanan and Tullock, 1962.) Constitutional choice is simply a choice of decision rules assigning decision-making capabilities among a community of people for making future decisions in the conduct of an organization or enterprise. Constitutional choice does not include the appropriation of funds or the taking of actions to alter events in the world except to provide a decision–making structure for ordering the choice of future decision makers. The organization of a public agency, when viewed as a problem in constitutional choice, is the choice or selection of an appropriate set of decision rules to be used in allocating decision-making capabilities among the community of people concerned with the provision of public goods and services under reasonably optimal conditions.

The rudiments of a theory of constitutional choice applicable to the organization of a public enterprise have been developed by James Buchanan and Gordon Tullock in *The Calculus of Consent* (1962). According to Buchanan and Tullock, a representative individual wanting to form an organization to provide a public good would need to take two types of costs into account: 1) external costs which are defined as those costs an individual would expect to bear as a result of decisions which deviate from his preferences and impose deprivations upon him; and 2) decision-making costs which are defined as the expenditure of resources, time, effort, and opportunities foregone in decision making. Both types of costs are affected by the selection of decision rules which specify the proportion of individuals required to agree prior to future collective action.

Expected external costs will be at their highest point where any *one* person can take action on behalf of the entire collectivity. Such costs would decline as the proportion of members participating in collective decision making increases. Expected external costs would reach zero where all were required to agree prior to collective action under a rule of unanimity. However, expected decision-making costs would have the opposite trend. Expenditures on decision making would be minimal if any *one* person could make future collective decisions for the whole group of affected individuals. Such costs would increase to their highest point with a rule of unanimity.

If a constitutional decision maker were a cost minimizer, and the two types of costs described above were an accurate representation of the costs he perceives, we would expect him to prefer the constitutional choice of a decision rule where the two cost curves intersect. When the two cost curves are roughly symmetrical, some form of simple majority vote would be a rational choice of a voting rule. If expected external costs were far greater than expected decision-making costs, an extraordinary majority would be a rational choice of a voting rule. Such a rule of extraordinary majority would presumably apply to the problem of constitutional choice where expected decision costs would be of minor magnitude providing that a reasonably optimal set of constitutional rules could be devised which would not impose high deprivations upon any particular element of the community. On the other hand, if the opportunity costs inherent in decision making were expected to be very large in comparison to external costs, then reliance might be placed on a rule authorizing collective action by the decision of one person in the extreme case requiring rapid response. (E. Ostrom, 1968.)

If the basic decision rules of a public or collective enterprise allowed for effective articulation of community preferences within agreeable decision rules, then advantage could be taken of any economies which might be realized through hierarchical control for organizing a production process capable of responding to community preferences. In turn, when collective provision of a public good of specifiable quality is undertaken, then each individual in that collectivity might rationally be assigned authority to require that his individual demands as a user of that good be met. Such a rule would specify the authority of *any one* to act in relation to his individual interest in the collective enterprise. An optimal set of decision rules for the constitution of public enterprises would be expected to vary with different situations. We would not expect to find one good rule that would apply to the provision of all types of public goods and services.

The similarity of these rules with elements in the structure of municipal corporations, public districts, and various local government agencies will be apparent to any student of American local government. If the rationale for such rules is theoretically sound, an appropriate structure of decision-making arrangements would exist which will require those in administrative responsibility to engage in an appropriate set of calculations and meet an appropriate set of conditions for sustaining public entrepreneurship under reasonably optimal conditions.

THE DEVELOPMENT OF
MULTI-ORGANIZATIONAL ARRANGEMENTS

The development of a self-governing public enterprise may not be a sufficient solution to problems of common pools or public goods. Several problems remain which may be sources of institutional weakness or institutional failure associated with such an enterprise. First, a public enterprise may generate externalities that impinge upon others *beyond its borders*. If the externalities are negative, means may be required to limit and control those externalities. If the externalities are positive, supplementary expenditures may be required to sustain an optimal yield of such externalities. Second, common properties or public goods may come in many different shapes and sizes with significant elements of jointness or interdependency among the various uses that can be made. Water resource systems, for example, reflect a baffling array of problems associated with persistent interdependencies among many joint uses. (V. Ostrom, 1968.) Interdependencies among water-related uses may also be interconnected with land use, energy supply systems, transport systems, etc. But each use may also involve independencies so that provision of a particular service will require separate consideration on its own merit. Third, where conflicts arise, institutional facilities need to be available for processing conflict and searching out resolutions that will preclude the tragedy of the commons from working itself out at some new level of interdependency. Multi-organizational arrangements can be conceptualized as a fourth type of institutional arrangements. As such it will involve a wide variety of inter-agency agreements and mechanisms for coping with inter-agency conflicts.

Some political economists have suggested that the problems arising from a great variety of public goods and services having many different sizes and shapes can be best resolved by taking advantage of the overlapping jurisdictions and fragmentation of authority inherent in the American political system. (Bish, 1971; Ostrom, Tiebout and Warren, 1961; Tiebout, 1956; Tullock, 1969.) Mancur Olson, for example, suggests:

> Only if there are several levels of government, and a large number of governments, can immense disparities between the boundaries of jurisdictions and the boundaries of collective goods be avoided. There is a case for every type of institution from the international organization to the smallest local government. It is the merit of the present approach that it can help explain the need for both centralized and decentralized units of government in the same context. [U. S. Congress, 1969:I, 327.]

This solution is the antithesis of that proposed in the classical public administration tradition. Instead of chaos and disorder, these political economists perceive a pattern of ordered relationships being sustained among diverse public enterprises.[11] Each different public enterprise is accountable to its relevant community of interests and functions essentially like a public firm in a much larger industrial complex. (V. Ostrom and E. Ostrom, 1965; V. Ostrom, 1969.)

Where externalities spill over into a larger domain and affect other closely associated uses, a second, third, and fourth level of organization can be relied upon to take care of those externalities that spill over from small-scale public jurisdictions. The first level agencies may, thus, operate as a small-scale producer and retailer in providing some public good or service to an immediate community of users. A second level of public agencies may function as intermediate producers and as wholesalers supplementing the operation of the first level agencies. The third and fourth level agencies may become large-scale producers providing a complement of services relevant to a much larger public domain.

If the first level agencies are constituted to articulate the preferences of the most immediate constituency of interests and are exposed to the demands of individual users, then such agencies can be expected to reflect those interests in bargaining with second, third, and fourth level agencies if substantial legal and political autonomy exists among the various public enterprises forming a public-service industry.

Once we begin to look for new patterns of order among the multi-organizational arrangements existing in a political economy characterized by overlapping jurisdictions and fragmentation of authority, we can begin to see that the American system of public education, the American highway system, the American police system, the American water resource system, and many other public service systems are operated by thousands of enterprises functioning at different levels of government. (V. Ostrom, 1969.) Each of these public service industries maintains and operates facilities serving diverse communities of interest. Despite the diversity of agencies

[71]

involved in the construction and maintenance of public roads, streets and highways, for example, the American highway system is a highly integrated network that has surprisingly few discontinuous or duplicate facilities.

As long as ample overlap and fragmentation of authority exist, agencies at one level of government can take advantage of the capabilities of agencies operating at other levels. (Landau, 1969.) If economies of scale in the production of a public good can be realized by a larger agency, smaller-sized agencies can enter into contractual arrangements to buy services from the larger agency. In such a circumstance small, local government agencies can operate as buyer's cooperatives on behalf of their constituents in arranging for the production of public services in accordance with the preferences of local inhabitants. (Ostrom, Tiebout and Warren, 1961.) A wide variety of municipal services, including police services, are now being provided as contract services in different metropolitan regions. We might anticipate that bilateral and multilateral bargaining will generate a higher level of efficiency in the provision of police services, for example, than is available in the very large, highly centralized, big city police departments. (E. Ostrom, *et al*, 1973.)

Conversely, if no economy of scale can be realized by increasing the size of the production unit, then the interests of the larger community of users can be accommodated by having the larger unit of government contract with the optimal scale producer to modify its facilities and services to accommodate the larger community of interests. The United States maintains an Interstate Highway System by contracting with state highway departments to plan, construct, and maintain highways in accordance with national standards and specifications. It is doubtful that the administration of the Interstate System would be improved by nationalizing all aspects of highway planning, construction, and maintenance.

[72]

Fiscal transfers from one level of government can be made to other levels of government where externalities accrue to a larger community of interest. Grants-in-aid are one method for accomplishing such transfers where smaller units, such as school districts, generate benefits which accrue to the nation as a whole. (Wagner, 1971.)

The industry characteristics of multi-organizational arrangements functioning in a public service economy can only be realized where diverse public agencies are able to develop different economies of scale in response to varying communities of interest. Overlapping jurisdictions and fragmentation of authority thus are necessary conditions for public services industries, other than fully integrated monopolies, to exist. Centralization cannot be conceived as the converse of decentralization in the sense that we speak of centralization *versus* decentralization. In responding to problems of diverse economies of scale, elements of centralization *and* decentralization must exist simultaneously among several jurisdictions with concurrent authority.[12]

The work of contemporary political economists, based upon a paradigm derived from economic theory, challenges many of the basic assumptions in the traditional theory of public administration. Yet, their form of analysis and many of their conclusions have a familiar ring to most Americans. This familiarity derives from the circumstance that many of the classical American political theorists were political economists and used a similar mode of analysis. (V. Ostrom, 1971a.) In the next lecture we shall use the intellectual perspective provided by contemporary political economists to examine the work of the classical political theorist. From this perspective, we shall discover that the classical political theorists have provided us with a theory of democratic administration which stands in contrast to the theory of bureaucratic administration.

[73]

A Theory of Democratic Administration:

the Rejected Alternative

Introduction

ONE OF THE MAJOR CONCLUSIONS DERIVED FROM THE from the political economists is that overlapping jurisdictions and fragmentation of authority can facilitate the production of a heterogeneous mix of public goods and services in a public service economy. This conclusion is contrary to the basic presumption in classical public administration theory that overlapping jurisdictions and fragmentation of authority are the principal source of institutional failure in American government.

The pioneer scholars in American public administration rested their political analysis upon a basic paradigmatic choice which explicitly rejected the political theory used in the design of the American constitutional system as being inappropriate for the study of political "realities." In this lecture I shall attempt to clarify the paradigmatic choice which Wilson made in pursuing his political analysis. I shall go behind that choice and examine the political theory which he rejected. In doing so, I shall advance the thesis that Wilson rejected a theory of democratic administration while propounding a theory of bureaucratic administration as the one rule of "good" administration for all governments alike.

Some Anomalous Threads of Thought

Wilson based his analysis upon a political science which derived its paradigm from Bagehot's *The English Constitution*. Wilson's reliance upon Bagehot led him to look for a single center of power in the American political system and to conclude that Congress was "the predominant and controlling force, the centre and source of all motive and of all regulative power" (Wilson, 1885:31.) in American government. His search for a single center of authority was based upon the assumption that:

> The natural, the inevitable tendency of every system of self-government like our own and the British is to exalt the representative body, the people's parliament, to a position of absolute supremacy. (Wilson, 1885:203.)

The exercise of "absolute supremacy" in a single center of authority is the essential feature of Thomas Hobbes' *Leviathan*. Bagehot and Wilson used an analytical paradigm similar to that of Hobbes for their political science.

Both Wilson and Bagehot, however, make anomalous allusions to the American constitutional system that are somewhat incongruous with the essential thrust of their analysis. Wilson, for example, concludes his essay on "The Study of Administration" by reference to "the systems within systems" that prevail in American government. (Wilson, 1887:221.) Local self-government is interlaced with self-government at the state and national levels. He then poses the question: "How shall our series of governments within governments be so administered that it shall always be to the interest of the public officer to serve, not his superior alone but the community as well, with the best efforts of his talents and the soberest

[75]

service of his conscience?" (Wilson, 1887:221.) This would imply that the decisions of a public officer are to be governed by his moral choice based upon considerations of conscience, the authority of political superiors, and the claims of the community as well. Such officers would indeed be governed by more than one master.

Bagehot, in turn, recognizes a basic difference in the conception of the English constitution as contrasted with the American constitution:

> In one the supreme determining power is upon all points the same; in the other that ultimate power is different upon different points—now resides in one part of the Constitution and now in another. (Bagehot, 1867:215.)

The English constitution was an example of the first type with "only one authority for all sorts of matters." The American constitution, by contrast, had "one ultimate authority for one sort of matter and another for another sort." Bagehot described the American political system as a *"composite"* type of government in contrast to the English system as a "simple" or unitary type. (Bagehot, 1867:219.)

Bagehot's references to the American constitutional system reflect substantial ambiguity on his part. He attributes the design of the American system to a misunderstanding of the English constitution which the Americans had attempted to copy in fashioning their own constitution. He has substantial doubts about the long-term viability of the American political system. "The practical arguments and legal disquisitions in America," reminded Bagehot of the problem confronting trustees in discharging a "misdrawn will." (Bagehot, 1867:218.) But Americans, like sensible trustees, could, according to Bagehot, make any constitution work. (Bagehot, 1867:220.) Yet, he concluded the introduction to his second edition by observing that the English constitution and the American constitution provide the two leading forms of "govern-ment by discussion." (Bagehot, 1867:310.) Government by discussion was, for Bagehot, a necessary condition for the development of a first-rate political community.

Rather than assume, like Bagehot, that the American constitutional system was based upon a misunderstand-ing of the English constitution, perhaps we should con-sider the possibility that the designers of the American constitution knew what they were doing and deliberately sought to base their political experiment upon an alterna-tive design. (V. Ostrom, 1971a.) In that case we would expect the American political system to reflect the par-ticular assumptions and concepts inherent in its design. Where those assumptions and concepts diverged from the English model, we would expect the American political system to generate quite different patterns of conduct from those generated by the English system. We might, for example, expect the federal structure of the American political system to be necessarily characterized by *over-lapping jurisdictions*. We might also expect a system of government which was designed to enforce provisions of constitutional law as against those who exercise govern-mental prerogative to be necessarily characterized by a separation of powers among diverse decision structures in the national government. A federal political system with substantial fragmentation of authority at each of the different levels of government would then be expected to maintain a diversity of public enterprises, each con-cerned with securing the support of its clientele or con-stituency and exposed to a variety of legislative, execu-tive, and judicial constraints. Together these diverse enterprises might be expected to develop multi-organizational structures analogous to public service industries.

We find some confirmation for these conjectures about varying design characteristics for different political

[77]

arrangements when we note that Max Weber associated bureaucratic administration with a system of rule based upon a "monocratic" principle. (Rheinstein, 1954:350.) A monocratic structure can be defined as one where all functionaries are integrated into a hierarchy culminating in a single center of ultimate authority. Unity of command is most fully attained in a monocratic system.

Weber also makes passing reference to a form of public administration which he calls "democratic administration" (Rheinstein, 1954:330–334.) in contrast to "bureaucratic administration." The defining characteristics of democratic administration for Weber are 1) an egalitarian assumption that everyone is qualified to participate in the conduct of public affairs and 2) the scope of the power of command is kept at a minimum. (Rheinstein, 1954:330.) Weber also indicates that "All important decisions are reserved to the common resolution of all." (Rheinstein, 1954:330.) Common resolution is attained through assemblies or collegial bodies which comprise or represent the members of a community or an organization. The administrative functionaries in such a democratic organization, Weber further notes, occupy a position that is "always in suspense between that of a mere servant and that of master." (Rheinstein, 1954:330.)

Democratic administration for Weber is *not* a viable alternative to bureaucratic administration. He dwells upon the limitations of democratic administration by indicating that it can apply only to local organizations or organizations with a limited number of members. Democratic administration is identified as a "marginal-type case," which cannot be treated as a *"historical starting point* of any typical [or general] course of development. . . ." (Rheinstein, 1954:331.) Weber could not contemplate the possibility that democratic administration might be juxtaposed to bureaucratic administration as an alternative model for the organization of public administration in a democratic society.

Perhaps both Weber and Wilson erred in failing to consider democratic administration to be a viable alternative to bureaucratic administration. When Alexis de Tocqueville visited America, he was much impressed with the system of administration that he found imbedded in democratic institutions.[1] Tocqueville undertook his study of *Democracy in America* (1835 and 1840) on the assumption that a great democratic revolution was sweeping through western civilization.[2] He was concerned that this revolution would generate a new democratic despotism which would enslave men and threaten the future of human civilization. Yet he saw hope in American democracy, especially in its structure of democratic administration.

Tocqueville recognized that this democratic revolution would require a "new science of politics" to assist in the governance of democratic societies if a new despotism were to be avoided. (Tocqueville, 1835 and 1840:I, 7.) He was concerned that individuals in a democratic society would "adopt the doctrine of self-interest" as their rule of action " *without understanding the science that puts it to use.*" (Tocqueville, 1835 and 1840:I, 11. My emphasis.) If men understood the science of how to put the doctrine of self-interest to proper use in governing society, Tocqueville could contemplate a society,

> in which all men would feel an equal love and respect for the laws of which they consider themselves the authors; in which the authority of the government would be respected as necessary, and not divine; and in which the loyalty of the subject to the chief magistrate would not be a passion but a quiet and rational persuasion. With every individual in the possession of rights which he is sure to retain, a kind of manly confidence and reciprocal courtesy would arise from

all classes removed alike from pride and servility. The people, well acquainted with their own interests, would understand that, in order to profit from the advantages of the state, it is necessary to satisfy its requirements. The voluntary association of citizens might then take the place of the individual authority of the nobles and the community would be protected from tyranny and license. (Tocqueville, 1835 and 1840:I, 9.)

Tocqueville's vision for a democratic society suggests that the American experiment might be viewed as a "historical starting point," to paraphrase Max Weber, in the development of a general system of democratic administration. Using Weber's defining characteristics, slightly modified, we would expect democratic administration to be based upon 1) an egalitarian assumption that everyone is qualified to participate in the conduct of public affairs, 2) the reservation of all important decisions for consideration by all members of the community and their elected representatives, 3) restriction of the power of command to a necessary minimum, and 4) modification of the status of administrative functionaries from that of masters to that of public servants. If a system of public administration having these characteristics can operate within a legal order subject to a rational rule of law and can provide public services as efficiently as a system of bureaucratic administration, then democratic administration need not be viewed as a "marginal-type case."

Democratic administration to be an *alternative* model to bureaucratic administration would also have to display such characteristics that we would be prepared to reject Wilson's basic thesis that there is but one rule of "good" administration for all governments alike. We would expect to find elements of bureaucratic organization; but we would not expect to find those elements to be the *dominant* characteristics in a system of democratic administration. Instead of a fully integrated structure of command, we would expect to find substantial dispersion of authority with many different structures of command. The exercise of control over the legitimate means of coercion would not be *monopolized* by a single structure of authority. Democratic administration would be characterized by *polycentricity* and *not* by *monocentricity*.

Our search for a democratic theory of administration will begin with the works that Wilson rejected in establishing the foundations for his political science. I shall look first at the works of Alexander Hamilton and James Madison in *The Federalist*. I shall then examine Tocqueville's commentary on democratic administration as contrasted to the patterns of bureaucratic administration found in France. French bureaucracy was Wilson's model of "good" administration.

Hamilton and Madison's Theory of Democratic Administration

Both Hamilton and Madison use the term democracy in a much more restricted sense than we use that term today. Madison, for example, defines democracy to be a society consisting of a small number of citizens who can assemble and directly administer their affairs in person. (*Federalist* 10.) However, both Hamilton and Madison make frequent reference to the term "popular" government. The word "popular" derives from a Latin root, *populus,* which has much the same meaning as the Greek root, *demos,* from which the term "democracy" derives. Both terms refer to people in the sense of a community of people. For our purposes, I assume that "popular" government is roughly equivalent to the modern meaning of "democratic" government. In this presentation, I shall use Max Weber's defining characteristics and measure the democratic theory of administration developed in *The Federalist* by those defining characteristics.

[81]

Most students of American public administration are thoroughly familiar with Hamilton's essay on the constitution of the executive department and on administration in *Federalist* 70 and *Federalist* 72.[3] Hamilton, in *Federalist* 70, indeed contends that, "Energy in the Executive is a leading character in the definition of good government." There he identifies unity in the executive as the first ingredient contributing to energy in the executive. By unity in the executive, Hamilton clearly means the exercise of control over the executive establishment in a single person as chief executive.

In *Federalist* 72, Hamilton addresses himself to the details of organization which fall within the province of the executive department. Executive responsibilities include such operations as foreign negotiations, preparing plans of finance, spending public monies in accordance with general appropriations of the legislature, organizing the army and navy, and directing the operations of war. In the discharge of these operations Hamilton observes:

> The persons ... to whose immediate management these different matters are committed ought to be considered as assistants or deputies of the chief magistrate, and on this account, they ought to derive their offices from his appointment, at least from his nomination, and ought to be subject to his superintendence. *(Federalist 72.)*

In these discussions of the national executive department, Hamilton's analysis relies upon a language which conforms closely to that of the traditional theory of public administration.

However, if we do *not* confine American public administration to the national executive department, we discover a different approach to problems of public administration in other portions of *The Federalist*. Extended commentaries on public administration are also found in Hamilton's analysis of problems of defense, internal security, and taxation. These commentaries use a language that is surprisingly similar to that of the contemporary political economists.

CONCURRENT ADMINISTRATION IN A FEDERAL SYSTEM

Hamilton's analysis of defense identifies the problem as one which is shared in common. Spanish and British territories surrounded the American states from Georgia to Maine. Both Spain and Britain were major maritime powers; and a future alliance between these two powers was possible. The danger was a common problem—a common threat to the security of the several states.

Hamilton asks whether the common defense should be secured by separate provision of the several states or by the common provision of the Union as a whole. If required to act under "the plan of separate provisions, New York," Hamilton observes, "would have to sustain the whole weight of the establishments requisite to her immediate safety, and to the mediate . . . protection of her neighbors." *(Federalist* 25.) Smaller states having less extensive commercial interests might in the short run rely for their security upon the defense measures of a stronger neighbor. The states shouldering a disproportionately large share of the burden for defense, according to Hamilton, "would be as little able as willing, for a considerable time to come, to bear the burden of competent provision." If the larger states, then, acted to reduce their burden, insufficient provision for the common defense would follow. "The security of all would thus be subjected to the parsimony, improvidence, or inability of a part." *(Federalist* 25.)

If the interests of the people in each state were purely defensive, the stronger states in providing for their own defense would assume a large part of the burden for protecting their weaker neighbors. The weaker neighbors, taking advantage of this opportunity, would make little

[83]

provision for defense and gain a comparative advantage by enjoying the protection of others without bearing their proportionate share of the costs. The people in the larger states, perceiving their plight in assuming a disproportionate share of the burden, would reduce their expenditures for defense. Thus, "the parsimony, improvidence, or inability" of each part to provide for the common good would lead to inadequate provision for the defense of the Union. *(Federalist* 25.)

If, however, two or three of the larger states were to assume a disproportionate share of the burden for defending American interests against external threat, those states need not limit their strategic opportunities to purely defensive actions. A disproportionately large military force in the command of two or three states might, Hamilton suggests, cause the other states to "quickly take alarm." Each would respond to the alarm by taking military countermeasures. Pretenses could easily be contrived to justify offensive action. And so,

> In this situation, military establishments, nourished by mutual jealousy, would be apt to swell beyond their natural or proper size; and being at the separate disposal of the members, they would be engines for the abridgement or demolition of the national authority. *(Federalist* 25.)

This type of analysis leads Hamilton to the conclusion that the proper means for guarding against a common danger "ought ... to be the objects of common councils and of a common treasury." *(Federalist* 25.) Congress would serve as a common council to authorize the creation of an appropriate force to assure the common defense of the American Union from resources provided by a common treasury contributed to by people in each of the various states through uniform measures of taxation.

Hamilton also recognized that each of the states would require the availability of a militia for its own internal security. In *Federalist* 29 Hamilton assumes the posture of advising a Federal legislator from his own state, New York, regarding the establishment of an appropriate mix of forces if the proposed constitution were ratified. Hamilton's optimal solution is a mixed force composed of 1) a select corps of well-trained militiamen in each state available a) for the defense of that state, or b) for mobilization by the United States for the common defense, and 2) a necessary complement of national forces to man frontier garrisons and to provide for the common defense of all of the states. The common defense and internal security of the United States would thus be provided by a combination of forces maintained by the coordinated actions of the states and national governments. This solution, Hamilton concluded, "appears to me the only substitute that can be devised for a standing army, and the best possible security against it, if it should exist." *(Federalist* 29.)

Both Hamilton and Madison further extend their argument to suggest that the existence of a militia in each of the states might also be used as a means of security against a military coup. Hamilton notes that people in a unitary or monocentric state, having no other institutions of government available to them, "can take no regular measures for defence" against a military coup.

The citizens must rush tumultously to arms, without concert, without system, without resource; except in their courage and despair. The usurpers, clothed with forms of legal authority, can too often crush the opposition in embryo. *(Federalist* 28.)

In a federal system of government with its overlapping jurisdictions, Madison anticipates quite a different outcome to any effort to usurp political authority by military force:

[T]he existence of subordinate governments, to which the people are attached, and by which the militia officers are appointed, forms a barrier against the enterprises of ambition, more insurmountable than any which a simple government of any form can admit ... [W]ere the people to possess the ... advantages of local governments chosen by themselves, who could collect the national will and direct the national force, and of officers appointed out of the militia, by these governments, and attached both to them and to the militia, it may be affirmed with the greatest assurance, that the throne of every tyranny in Europe would be speedily overturned in spite of the legions which surround it. *(Federalist* 46.)

A federal system with its concurrent regimes or overlapping jurisdictions provides Madison with the happy circumstances that "the great and aggregate interests" of the American people could be organized in relation to a national government where the local and particular interests could be organized into numerous state and local governments. Madison was persuaded that "[I]t is only in a certain sphere that federal power can, in the nature of things, be advantageously administered." Presumably "the nature of things" reflects events of diverse sizes and shapes. Jurisdictions of different scale can advantageously administer programs capable of dealing with differently sized events. "The federal and State governments are ... but different agents and trustees of the [same] people, constituted with different powers and designed for different purposes." *(Federalist* 46.) Madison is not especially disturbed about the prospect of a rivalry between Federal and state agencies for popular support:

If ... the people should ... become more partial to the federal than to the State governments, the change can only result from such manifest and irresistible proofs of a better administration as will overcome all their antecedent propensities [to favor the states.] [T]he people ought not ... be precluded from giving most of their confidence where they may discover it to be the most due ... *(Federalist* 46.)

In a federal system with its concurrent structures of governmental authority, Hamilton is generally persuaded that the people can be masters of their own fate by using one system of government to check the usurpations of the other.

The people, by throwing themselves into either scale, will infallibly make it preponderate. If their rights are invaded by either, they can make use of the other as the instrument of redress ... *(Federalist* 28.)

In his analysis of the concurrent powers of taxation shared by the state and national governments, Hamilton rejects the assumption that a fully duplicate and separable system of tax administration will be established. Instead, he suggests that the national administration will work out cooperative arrangements with the states so that each can gain the advantage of joint action and avoid the prospects of mutually exclusive rivalry. Thus, he anticipates that "The national legislature can make use of the *system of each State within that State." (Federalist* 36. Hamilton's emphasis.) The use of the system internal to each state as an adjunct to national administration becomes readily available so long as the state does not possess a formal veto on national programs and so long as the national legislature has the independent authority to devise its own system of administration. Both are free to consider cooperative arrangements so long as each is free to consider alternative forms of action. Hamilton clearly anticipated the possibility of fiscal transfers occurring between different units of government to facilitate coordinated arrangements where one unit of government can take advantage of the capabilities afforded by other units of government. *(Federalist* 36.)

The system of administration which Hamilton and Madison envisioned in the American federal system was to operate in the context of a political system in which *all* units of government were to be fashioned upon principles of self-government. *(Federalist* 39.) While Hamilton and Madison do not at any one place specifically enumerate the principles of self-government, the following principles discussed at various places in *The Federalist* might be included as among the principles of self-government applicable to each unit of government:

First, terms and conditions of government derive from the right of the people to establish and alter those terms and conditions. *(Federalist* 40.)

Second, the right of the people to establish and alter the terms and conditions of government is expressed through processes of constitutional decision making which require action by extraordinary decision rules. These decision rules have more demanding requirements than those necessary to enact ordinary legislation. *(Federalist* 39.)

Third, the terms and conditions of government specified in a constitution or a charter are legally binding upon those who exercise governmental authority and are unalterable by those governmental authorities. *(Federalist* 53.)

Fourth, the terms and conditions of government specified in a constitution or a charter assign both authority to act on behalf of the commonweal and limitations upon that authority. Limitations upon the authority of public officials to take collective action are specified as correlative rights of persons which establish constitutional grounds for individual actions against the usurpation of public authority. *(Federalist* 78.)

Fifth, each unit of government acts in relation to a defined constituency and exercises its jurisdiction in relation to persons as individuals. The selection of principal governmental officials responsible for taking legislative or executive action is based upon either direct or indirect election of constituents. *(Federalist* 10, 16, 35, and 57–59.)

Sixth, the internal structure of each unit of government is devised so that collective decision making is allocated among diverse positions or decision structures. All important decisions are subject to considerations by the common council of those who depend upon election by members of the community. Dispersion of authority among diverse decision structures in any one unit of government is a necessary condition if the rules of constitutional law are to be enforceable as against those who exercise governmental authority. *(Federalist* 47 and 80.)

Seventh, the authority allocated to the diverse decision structures in the larger units of governments is so divided that each is able to exercise potential veto positions in relation to the authority allocated to others. Collective action thus depends upon the operation of concurrent majorities exercised by decision structures which are composed of members who are related to their constituencies through varying terms of office, modes of representation, and differently sized constituencies. *(Federalist* 51–52, 56–58, and 73.)

Eighth, the legal and political competence of each unit of government is limited in relation to the legal and political competence of other units of government. Each person is a constituent member of several units of government. Local and state officials will act in relation to national problems; national officials will act in relation to state and local problems. Where the domain of a smaller unit of government is insufficient to take account of the common interest among interdependent events, reference can be taken to the next larger unit to secure an appropriate scale of decision making. *(Federalist* 10, 16, 46, and 51.)

Ninth, conflicts over jurisdiction among units of government, conflicts over constitutional limits upon the exercise of public authority, and conflicts over the provision of public services are all subject to judicial remedies before the regular courts of law. *(Federalist* 80.)

These principles of self-government are highly consistent with Max Weber's defining characteristics of democratic administration. Weber's egalitarian assumption that everyone is qualified to participate in the conduct of public affairs is reflected in conditions where members of the community at large are presumed to have an important voice in constitutional decision making, to elect public officials, and to hold those officials individually accountable for expressing the essential interests of constituents in major decisions. Individuals also have the prerogative to press for the enforcement of demands upon public officials through administrative, legislative, judicial, political, and constitutional remedies. Important decisions are reserved for consideration by members of the community and by their elected representatives. The power of command is severely restricted by the scrutiny of officials in diverse decision structures within any particular unit of government, by the allocation of authority among different units of government, and by the presumption that the exercise of all governmental authority is limited by the terms and conditions specified in constitutional law. Finally, these various control mechanisms imply that administrative officials are obliged to *serve* members of the community rather than function as their masters.

In general, we might conclude that the principles of self-government discussed in *The Federalist* provide for a system of administration which is thoroughly imbedded in a complex structure of democratic decision making. The American experiment can be viewed as a "historical starting point" for a generic type of administration to be characterized as "democratic" administration in contrast to "bureaucratic" administration. Hamilton's theory of administration in *Federalist* 70 and 72 might then be considered as a *special* theory of administration applicable to the Federal executive structure but *not* applicable to the American system of government as a whole. The general conditions of hierarchical ordering within a bureaucratic system of administration can be significantly relaxed if public administration is organized in relation to the specific constituencies being served and if mechanisms of popular control, legislative surveillance, and judicial remedies are substituted for mechanisms of bureaucratic control. Processes of democratic administration necessarily depend upon mechanisms for democratic control being operable in the conduct of any public enterprise.[4]

Tocqueville's Analysis of Democratic Administration

Tocqueville, in *Democracy in America,* focuses his attention primarily upon the conditions of political organization within what he called the American "republics." His concern is primarily with the American states and with the systems of government within each state. He gives relatively less attention to the constitution of the national government and to its place in American society. Tocqueville's work thus provides an important complement to *The Federalist* in elucidating the political system within states rather than the relationship of the Union to the states.

Tocqueville recognizes that the American tradition of self-government grew out of the townships, took possession of the states, and then fashioned a national constitution predicated upon those republican principles which were current in the whole community before the constitution existed. (Tocqueville, 1835 and 1840:I, 59.) The American constitution is a complex system which, according to Tocqueville,

consists of two distinct social structures connected, and, as it were, encased one within the other; two governments, completely separate and almost independent, the one fulfilling

[91]

the ordinary duties and responding to the daily and indefinite calls of a community, the other circumscribed within certain limits and only exercising an exceptional authority over the general interest of the country. In short, there are twenty-four small sovereign nations, whose agglomeration constitutes the body of the Union. (Tocqueville, 1835 and 1840:I, 59.)

Tocqueville characterizes the political and administrative affairs of each state as being "centered in three foci of action:" the township, the county, and the state. (Tocqueville, 1835 and 1840:I, 59–60.) Each is governed on the principle that "everyone (i.e., every individual) is the best and sole judge of his own private interest, and that society has no right to control a man's actions unless they are prejudicial to the common weal or unless the common weal demands his help." (Tocqueville, 1835 and 1840:I, 64.) The township in turn is independent in all that concerns itself alone and is subordinate to the state only in those interests that are shared in common. These principles are applicable to each of the several foci of action or centers of authority which are available to each citizen in governing the diverse communities of interests which he shares with others in his town, his county, his state and his nation.

The reiteration of the principles of self-government in each different unit of government means that public administration is confined to circumstances where centralization and hierarchy can be held to a minimum. Instead of a single hierarchy of public functionaries, Tocqueville found that "the executive power is disseminated into a multitude of hands." (Tocqueville, 1835 and 1840:I, 81.) People participate in the execution of their laws by the choice of public executives as well as in the making of their laws through the choice of legislators. Political responsibility is secured *more* by the principles of election than by accountability to central authority through a single hierarchy of control. Popular political control pervades both the government *and* its administration.

Tocqueville recognizes that the use of popular elections to choose public officers, who are responsible for the execution of the law and for the discharge of public services, creates a problem of how to compel popularly elected officials to conform to the law. He found that conflicts among independently elected administrative officials are resolved by adjudication of the courts of law. "The courts of justice ... alone can compel the elected functionaries to obey, without violating the rights of the electors." (Tocqueville, 1835 and 1840:I, 74.) Where elections, instead of the authority of command in a single administrative hierarchy, are the primary method for the control of administration, Tocqueville concludes that:

> The extension of judicial power in the political world ought to be in the exact ratio as the extension of the elective power; if these two institutions do not go hand in hand, the state must fall into anarchy or into servitude. (Tocqueville, 1835 and 1840:I, 74.)

As republican institutions are replicated in multitudinous units of governments serving as many different communities of interest, a rule of law can be sustained as conflicts between individual citizens and public officials or among public officials in different jurisdictions are adjudicated by courts of law. As Tocqueville noted, "In no country in the world does the law hold so absolute a language as in America; and in no country is the right of applying it vested in so many hands." (Tocqueville, 1835 and 1840:I, 71) Thus, the legal basis of a rational social order can be sustained by reliance upon the offices of the judiciary as well as by reference to administrative functionaries in a Weberian bureaucracy.

[93]

The mandate of executive leadership can thus be constrained by popular election, legislative surveillance, and judicial remedies. Under such circumstances, elected executives can be required to function as public servants in their communities rather than as the political masters over those communities. Americans have recourse to some 80,000 hierarchies of diverse sizes rather than to a single overarching hierarchy of public authority.

The essential spirit of American democracy, for Tocqueville, is reflected in a system of democratic administration organized primarily by principles of voluntary association and principles of self-government. As a European observer, Tocqueville noted that "The appearance of disorder which prevails on the surface leads one to imagine that society is in a state of anarchy...." (Tocqueville, 1835 and 1840:I, 89.) But a deeper look revealed an underlying order in the bustle of activity:

> In America the power that conducts the administration is far less regular, less enlightened, and less skillful, but a hundredfold greater than in Europe. In no country in the world do the citizens make such exertions for the common weal. I know of no people who have established schools so numerous and efficacious, places of public worship better suited to the wants of the inhabitants, or roads kept in better repair. Uniformity or permanence of design, the minute arrangement of details, and the perfection of administrative system must not be sought for in the United States; what we find is the presence of a power which, if it is somewhat wild, is at least robust, and an existence checkered with accidents, indeed, but full of animation and effort. (Tocqueville, 1835 and 1840:I, 91–92.)

The uniformity of design, the minute arrangement of detail, and the perfection of administration associated with centralized administration in France had the opposite effect. "[I]t excels in prevention but not in action." (Tocqueville, 1835 and 1840:I, 90.) The citizen in a centralized state would rather become "a passive spectator than a dependent actor in schemes with which he is unacquainted." (Tocqueville, 1835 and 1840:I, 91.) Perfection in centralized administration will lead to tranquility without happiness, industry without improvement, stability without strength, and public order without public morality. (Tocqueville, 1835 and 1840:I, 90.) It is in such circumstances that ordinary citizens become indifferent to the interest of the community in which they live. (Tocqueville, 1856:44.)

If egalitarian conditions of life characteristic of democratic societies were combined with a highly centralized system of administration, Tocqueville anticipated that such societies would include:

> an innumerable multitude of men, all equal and all alike, incessantly endeavoring to procure the petty and paltry pleasures with which they glut their lives. Each of them, living apart, is a stranger to the fate of the rest; his children and his private friends constitute to him the whole of mankind. As for the rest of his fellow citizens, he is close to them, but he does not see them; he touches them, but he does not feel them; he exists only in himself and for himself alone.... (Tocqueville, 1835 and 1840:II, 318.)

Above this multitude of men Tocqueville sees:

> an immense and tutelary power which takes upon itself alone to secure their gratification and to watch over their fate. That power is absolute, minute, regular, provident and mild.... [I]t chooses to be the sole agent and the only arbiter of [their] happiness; it provides for their security; foresees and supplies their necessities, facilitates their pleasures, manages their principal concerns, directs their industry, regulates the descent of property, and subdivides their inheritance: what remains, but to spare them all the care of thinking and all the trouble of living. (Tocqueville, 1835 and 1840:II, 318.)

[I]t compresses, ennervates, extinguishes and stupefies a people, till each nation is reduced to nothing better than a flock of timid and industrious animals, of which the government is the shepherd. (Tocqueville, 1835 and 1840:II, 319.)

Such is Tocqueville's view of democratic society with a centralized government and a bureaucratic administration. The fully developed bureaucracy in a democratic society will generate, as Tocqueville foresees, a "species of oppression" which "is unlike anything that ever before existed in our world; our contemporaries will find no prototype of it in their memories." (Tocqueville, 1835 and 1840:II, 318.)

Tocqueville would certainly have rejected Wilson's theory of administration that there is but one rule of good administration for all governments alike. An "ultra-monarchial form of administration" combined with a republican constitution could only be a shortlived monster for Tocqueville. (Tocqueville, 1835 and 1840:II, 321.) Mass societies dominated by highly centralized bureaucratic structures were the essential attributes of a new species of oppression that Tocqueville envisioned for the future of mankind.[5]

Tocqueville was persuaded that a large democratic society could be free *only* if men comprehend the *utility* of political forms or of political structures in the constitution of democratic governments. He would certainly have agreed with Weber that a democratic system of administration in a free society must be based upon 1) an egalitarian assumption that everyone is qualified to participate in the conduct of public affairs, 2) the reservation of all important decisions for consideration by all members of the community and their elected representatives, 3) restriction of the power of command to a minimum, and 4) modification of the status of administrative functionaries from that of masters to that of public servants.

Such possibilities can only be realized where careful attention is given to political forms which allow for concurrent action in several overlapping jurisdictions or concurrent foci of action:

> Municipal institutions constitute the strength of free nations. Town meetings are to liberty what primary schools are to science: they bring it within the people's reach, they teach men how to use and enjoy it. (Tocqueville, 1835 and 1840:I, 61.)

Under these circumstances, Tocqueville indicates elsewhere that in a free democratic society "every man is daily reminded of the need of meeting his fellow men, of hearing what they have to say, of exchanging ideas, and coming to an agreement as to the conduct of their common interests. (Tocqueville, 1856, xiv.)

Restriction of the power of command also depends upon the fragmentation of authority among decision structures if the discretion of officials is to be limited by a rule of law. The power of the courts, in particular, must grow in proportion to the increase in popular control if democratic administration is to be the basis for a rational legal order. (Tocqueville, 1835 and 1840:I, 74.) In short, Tocqueville anticipated that liberty could be sustained in an egalitarian society only if a system of public administration were developed which would meet the defining criteria used by Max Weber in characterizing democratic administration. *Democratic administration cannot be separated from the processes of popular control inherent in democratic politics.*

The work of Hamilton and Madison and of Tocqueville involves the articulation of a theory of democratic administration when measured in terms of the criteria specified by Max Weber. The American experiment, based upon a theory of democratic administration, can thus be viewed as a turning point in pioneering a new course of human development. Democratic administration, through a system of overlapping jurisdictions and fragmentation of authority, acquired a stable form which provides an alternative structure for the organization of public administration. Democratic administration need not be a "marginal-type case" confined only to local organizations with a limited number of members. A democratic theory of administration is the approach that Wilson rejected while propounding a bureaucratic theory of administration as being universally applicable to all systems of modern government. We shall pursue some of the implications of a theory of democratic administration for the study of public administration in the concluding lecture.

The Choice of Alternative Futures

Some Opportunity Costs in the Choice of Paradigm

IN THE COURSE OF THESE LECTURES, WE HAVE EXAMINED the study of public administration from an assumption that the persisting intellectual crisis is a paradigmatic crisis as conceptualized by Thomas Kuhn in his *Structure of Scientific Revolutions*. We have argued that Woodrow Wilson and his contemporaries made an explicit paradigmatic choice in rejecting the political theory articulated by Hamilton and Madison in *The Federalist*.[1] The political theory in *The Federalist* was dismissed as having no analytical relevance for understanding the "realities" of American politics except to explain the source of some of the pathologies in American government. That theory, according to Wilson, had "proved mischievous" just to the extent that it had succeeded in establishing itself in practice. (Wilson, 1885:187.)

Wilson's analytical theory assumed that the natural and inevitable tendency in any system of government is to have recourse to some sovereign body which will exercise "ultimate supremacy" and have the last say in making collective decisions. It is in this sense that we speak of a government as having a monopoly over the legitimate exercise of authority in a society. Indeed, much of contemporary political science is based upon this presumption.

In such a theory, the distinguishing feature of a democratic or republican form of government is whether ultimate authority is exercised by a representative assembly selected by vote of the people. Thus, Wilson simply took it for granted that, "the representatives of the people are the proper ultimate authority in all matters of government, and that the administration is merely the clerical part of government." (Wilson, 1885:181.) Wilson saw good administration as a single hierarchical arrangement generic to all forms of government. The constitution of different governments might vary in form; but the pattern of good administration will always be of the same form.

The choice of a paradigm in public administration depends upon the relative advantage which can be derived from a reliance upon one or another approach. To estimate the relative advantage inherent in different approaches, we must clarify basic assumptions about the nature of political organization and determine the consequences which are likely to follow from relying upon differently designed structures or organizational relationships. If our calculation of the consequences which follow from differently designed organizational arrangements are well founded, then each person can estimate the costs which are inherent in the opportunities which would be foregone by taking one or another approach. He can assess the differences in opportunities foregone in arriving at his own assessment of the opportunity costs inherent in a choice of paradigm.

A Theory of Sovereign Prerogative

The basic theory of sovereignty inherent in Wilson's political science was formulated by Thomas Hobbes.

Hobbes reasoned that, in the absence of some superior power, the natural condition of man was a state of war in which each man was potentially exposed to acts of violence by every other man. In order to enjoy the felicity of a state of peace, men must be prepared to forego some options and agree to carry on relationships under terms and conditions that would not cause harm or injury to others. Hobbes was able to conceptualize the axioms for a felicitous order or a state of peace. However, he argued that these axioms were insufficient for a stable commonwealth in the absence of a commanding power to enforce such axioms as rules of law. In Hobbes' words, "covenants, without the sword, are but words." (Hobbes, 1651:109.) Laws to be effective depend upon mechanisms for their enforcement.

For there to be one society there must in Hobbes' theory be one system of law. For there to be one system of law, there must be but one source of law. Since the substance of law is established by its enforcement, there can only be one ultimate source of authority in both the formulation and the enforcement of law. Thus, Hobbes envisioned a unification of the offices of legislation, of administration, and of adjudication in relation to a single sovereign with ultimate authority over all governmental prerogatives. A unitary sovereign was, he assumed, a necessary condition for maintaining a lawful and stable commonwealth. Such a sovereign is the source of law and cannot be held accountable to any rule of law. Thus, the sovereign is above the law. The price of peace is deference and obedience to the authority of an absolute sovereign. Obedience is the essential virtue for good administration in a Hobbesian commonwealth.

Wilson's adherence to a unitary theory of sovereign prerogative led to his rejection of *The Federalist* as a political theory based upon division of authority or separation of powers. In rejecting *The Federalist,* Wilson was rejecting the theory which was used to articulate the design of the American political system. An appropriate theory of design is necessary both to understand how a system will work and how modifications or changes in a system will affect its performance. To use one theory of design to evaluate the characteristics of a system based upon a different theory of design can lead to profound misunderstandings. To use one theory of design to reform a system based upon a different theory of design may produce many unanticipated and costly consequences. A Volkswagen is not a Ford. To evaluate one by the design criteria of the other or to repair one by using the parts of the other would not be reasonable procedures.

A THEORY OF POSITIVE CONSTITUTIONAL LAW

The theory of design used by the Americans in fashioning their constitution was of a radically different magnitude than the theory of design that Wilson used in his evaluation of that system. The Americans sought to fashion a system of government where those who exercised the prerogatives of government would have limited authority subject to the terms and conditions of constitutional law. The design for the American political system was based upon a theory of positive (that is, enforceable) constitutional law.[2] Hobbes considered such a theory to be repugnant to the nature of commonwealths. (Hobbes, 1651:ch. 26, and 212–213.) Who is to enforce the law upon those who have the ultimate authority and exercise a monopoly over the legitimate use of coercive capabilities in a society? The sovereign is the source of law and cannot be held accountable to the law.

Perhaps in light of nearly two centuries of experience, we can begin to contemplate the possibility that the American experiment was not a fundamental error or misunderstanding based upon "paper pictures" or "literary theories." (Wilson, 1885:31.) Instead, the American experiment reflects a different theory of design than Hobbes' *Leviathan*. (V. Ostrom, 1971a.) A key to understanding the design of the American political system is to specify the logically necessary conditions for a system of positive constitutional law which is enforceable as against those who exercise governmental prerogatives.[3]

Several conditions would appear to be logically necessary for a system of positive constitutional law:

First, a system of positive constitutional law will necessarily depend upon processes of constitutional decision making which exist, at least in part, outside the competence of governmental authorities who are subject to its provisions. A positive constitution must be *unalterable* by governmental authorities acting upon their own motions if such authorities are to be limited in their decision-making capabilities. *(Federalist 53.)*

Second, a system of positive constitutional law will necessarily depend upon a separation of powers so that each set of governmental decision makers will act in relation to limits placed upon their authority by other sets of governmental officials. (Vile, 1967: 310.) Some form of separation of powers, or fragmentation of authority, thus, is a logically necessary condition for enforcing provisions of constitutional law as against governmental decision makers. *(Federalist 47.)*

Third, a system of legally enforceable constitutional law will necessarily depend upon an explicit formulation of the constitutional authority of persons in terms of rights which are not subject to alienation (that is, cannot be alienated, transferred, or taken away) by governmental authorities. The constitutional authority of persons creates correlative limits upon the authority of those who exercised governmental prerogatives. Persons will then be able to exercise constitutional authority in asserting their claims as against governmental decision makers.

Fourth, a system of positive constitutional law will also depend upon citizens who are prepared to pay the price of civil disobedience in being willing to challenge the constitutional validity of any law or official action, and face punishment and official displeasure if their cause is not affirmed. Persons in a constitutional republic must be able to initiate and sustain causes of action in the protection of their constitutional rights and in the imposition of limits upon governmental authorities. The constitutional office of *persons* assumes substantial significance in the maintenance of a lawful constitutional order. We might, then, assume that the ultimate authority to deal with the jurisdiction of government rests broadly in all of those who function as members in such a political community and share a common theory of constitutional law.

Finally, a positive constitutional law will depend upon the existence of alternative political regimes each with its own charter or constitution so that individuals can have access to different units of government to articulate diverse communities of interest. Each individual will have access to alternative regimes and to the political, judicial, and constitutional remedies afforded by those diverse regimes. Conflicts of interest can be articulated in diverse forums. The action of officials in each regime will serve to establish limits upon the exercise of discretion by those who act on behalf of other regimes.

Specification of logically necessary conditions for a positive constitutional law does *not,* however, provide us with both the necessary and *sufficient* conditions for a positive constitutional law. The choice of political arrangements is within the domain of choice. Human discretion can be exercised at variance with decision rules. Madison recognized this condition when he observed that, "In every political institution, a power to advance the public happiness involves a discretion which may be misapplied and abused." *(Federalist* 41.)

The selection of decision rules for inclusion within a constitution is based upon estimates of the probable consequences that constitutional decision makers expect to flow from different decision rules. The success of constitutional decision making, thus, depends upon a knowledge of the probable consequences which will flow from different decision rules. Such knowledge will always be subject to conditions of risk and uncertainty. The long-term viability of the American constitutional system will depend upon the capability of the American people to 1) provide remedies as against those who usurp authority and abuse their public trust and 2) reform the structure of government so as to maintain the essential equilibrium of a system of constitutional rule.

The successful reform of the American constitutional system requires a continued knowledge of the probable consequences flowing from different decision rules. This knowledge must include an assessment of the costs as well as the benefits which are necessarily associated with any particular constitutional design. Such costs can be minimized but never eliminated. It is not possible to gain the benefits of constitutional rule without reaping its disadvantages as well. An absence of knowledge about the costs inherent in the design of any particular political system may lead individuals to attempt reforms which are aimed at eliminating those costs. Attempts to eliminate costs inherent in the design of any system may lead to its impairment and to an elimination of the benefits which accrue from that system.

Some Necessary Costs of a System of Positive Constitutional Law

A political system which is designed to enforce a system of positive constitutional law as against one which is designed to articulate the exercise of a unitary sovereignty will necessarily involve costs in delay, open controversy, and complex relationships. Hamilton, for example, recognized that the power "of preventing bad laws" inherent in the exercise of veto capabilities also involves the power "of preventing good ones." However, he also contends that "[T]he oftener [a] measure is brought under examination, the greater the diversity of situations of those who are to examine it, the less will be the danger of those errors which flow from want of due deliberation." (*Federalist* 73.) Thus, the costs of delay need to be weighed as against the costs of errors engendered by hasty action. Similarly, the costs of open controversy must be weighed against the costs of secret cabals.

Tocqueville is also quite explicit in warning his European compatriots about the complexity of the American political system and the relatively high level of knowledge required to pursue strategic opportunities in that system. Yet that cost must be weighed against the danger that simple solutions will lead to the concentration of political power in a single center of authority. Tocqueville would have concurred with Justice Story's observation that,

> In proportion as a government is free, it must be complicated. Simplicity belongs to those only where one will govern all ... , where law is not a science but a mandate to be followed and not to be discussed.[4]

A Science of Association as Knowledge of Form and Reform

Tocqueville has suggested that the danger of democratic despotism engendered by the search for simple solutions in a centralized state can be avoided if a democratic people give proper attention to political science as a "science of association." He views a science of association as being "the mother of sciences" in democratic countries: "the progress of all else depends upon the progress it has made." (Tocqueville, 1835 and 1840:II, 110.) A science of association will enable men in a democratic society to "comprehend the utility of forms" (Tocqueville, 1835 and 1840:II, 325) for putting the doctrine of self-interest to proper use as a rule of action for organizing and sustaining collective enterprises. (Tocqueville, 1835 and 1840:I, 10.) Tocqueville observes that, "If men are to remain civilized or to become so, the art of associating together must grow and improve in the same ratio in which the equality of conditions is increased." (Tocqueville, 1835 and 1840:II, 110.) A science of association is a necessary ingredient for advancing civilization in democratic societies and is the basis for Tocqueville's conclusion that "A new science of politics is needed for a new world." (Tocqueville, 1835 and 1840:I, 7.)

It is precisely this science of association and the art of associating together that is the critical issue in the study of public administration. Those who study, teach, and practice public administration must come to some basic resolutions about the essential relationship between conditions and consequences for constituting and reforming human associations. Must the science of association utilized in public administration be built upon a Hobbesian theory of sovereignty? Or can a science of association also be built upon a theory of limited constitutions on the assumption that political structures can be devised in which those who exercise the extraordinary prerogatives of government are subject to the rule of constitutional law?

SOME COMMON ASSUMPTIONS

It can be argued that both Hobbes' theory of sovereignty and the American theory of a limited constitution are based upon some initial assumptions that are common to both. Hamilton and Madison rely upon a model man that is fully consistent with Hobbes' model of man as formulated in his essay "Of Men" in the *Leviathan*. Both view social organization as being grounded in a structure of enforceable legal relationships. The distinguishing characteristic of government is its power to enforce law. To that extent, both are based upon a common science of human association. The assumptions common to both include the following:

First, individual human beings are assumed to be the basic material or units which form any political system. No government will exist without reference to individual human beings. Each person, in the final analysis, is assumed to be the judge of his own self-interest and can be expected to act in a way that will enhance his net welfare potential.

Second, decision rules are the basis for ordering relationships in any association. Decision rules are propositions assigning decision-making capabilities to those who participate in social relationships. Limiting the field of choice by recourse to decision rules is a necessary condition for establishing predictability in social relationships. Discretion exercised in accordance with decision rules will allow pursuit of some possibilities and exclude other possibilities. If actions injurious to others can be excluded from the domain of choice, then human welfare would be enhanced by the pursuit of lawful possibilities.

Third, decision rules are neither self-generating nor self-modifying, but depend upon individual persons both for their formulation and alteration. If persons are to act consistently and productively in relation to one another, then means must be available for constraining and resolving conflicts which arise from actions taken in accordance with existing decision rules and for devising new decision rules to comprehend new social conditions.

Fourth, decision rules are not self-enforcing but depend upon the assignment of extraordinary powers to *some* persons to enforce decision rules in relation to other members of a community. Such powers include the capacity to impose coercive sanctions and thus involve the potential use of lawful decision-making capabilities to impose deprivations upon others.

Fifth, given the conditions specified in the above assumptions, then we must necessarily conclude that any form of organization capable of establishing and enforcing ordered social relationships among a large community of persons will necessarily depend upon a *radical inequality* in the assignment of decision-making capabilities to those who exercise the prerogatives for allocating and controlling the decision-making capabilities exercised by others. *Conditions of political inequality must necessarily exist in any political association.* (V. Ostrom, 1971a:27.)

Two Different Solutions to the Problem of Political Inequality

Hobbes' theory of sovereignty and the American theory of the limited constitution depart from one another as each provides a *different* solution to the problem of political inequality. Hobbes accepts political inequality as a necessary and sufficient condition for the organization of any commonwealth: there must be *a* commanding power! Peace can be maintained in a society only if inequality is absolute. There must be a single center of authority capable of exercising *absolute* sovereignty if a stable and peaceful commonwealth is to be maintained. The price of peace is obedience to the sovereign; the sovereign is the source of law; and the sovereign is above the law.

The Americans were concerned with the problem of whether societies of men could, by reflection and choice, institute a system of government where constitutional law could be used to enforce limits upon those who exercise the prerogatives of government. The condition of political inequality need not be absolute but only sufficient to maintain the enforceability of commonly accepted rules of law. Power can be divided and arranged among the several offices of government in such a manner that each will be a check upon the other. By connecting the interest of the man to the constitutional authority of the office, ambition can be made to counteract ambition. Agreement will prevail where benefits accrue from mutual advantage. Conflict will intervene when some seek an advantage at the expense of others. Political structures are but a method for encapsulating conflict while due deliberation is sustained until human reason can search out new and improved solutions. The U. S. Constitution is an effort to provide for a system of rule where rulers are themselves subject to the rule of law.

If we assume that each theoretical formulation has the potential for being logically sound and operationally feasible, we would expect the two formulations to reflect quite different design characteristics. We would further expect those design characteristics to be organized through different decision structures and to give rise to quite different sets of consequences when implemented in an operable system of government. (V. Ostrom, 1971a.) These consequences will include both benefits *and* costs. Every choice has its price.

From this analysis, we would expect Wilson's theory of administration to be relevant for a political system with a highly centralized monocentric decision structure. His theory would be appropriate for understanding and reforming the French and Prussian political systems or those having similar structural characteristics. Conversely, we would *not* expect Wilson's theory to apply to a highly polycentric political system with substantial overlapping of jurisdictions and fragmentation of authority. We would then be led to reject Wilson's thesis that there is but one rule of good administration for *all* governments alike. We would also entertain the possibility that the American experiment represents a "historical starting point" of major significance in the development of a system of democratic administration. Democratic administration as a general form of public administration can be juxtaposed to bureaucratic administration as an alternative type.

Basic Propositions in a Paradigm of Democratic Administration

The basic propositions inherent in the paradigm that Wilson proposed to use for building a science of administration were summarized in the second lecture. (See *supra,* pp. 28–29.) The basic propositions relating to a science of democratic administration inherent in a paradigm which grows out of the work of the modern political economists and the work of classical democratic theorists can be summarized as follows:

1. Individuals who exercise the prerogatives of government are no more nor no less corruptible than their fellow men.

2. The exercise of political authority—a necessary power to do good—will be usurped by those who perceive an opportunity to exploit such powers to their own advantage and to the detriment of others unless authority is divided and different authorities are so organized as to limit and control one another.

3. The structure of a constitution allocates decision-making capabilities among a community of persons; and a democratic constitution defines the authority inherent in both the prerogatives of persons and in the prerogative of different governmental offices so that the capabilities of each are limited by the capabilities of others. The task of establishing and altering organizational arrangements in a democratic society is to be conceived as a problem in constitutional decision making.[5]

4. The provision of public goods and services depends upon decisions taken by diverse sets of decision makers and the political feasibility of each collective enterprise depends upon a favorable course of decisions in all essential decision structures over

[111]

time. Public administration lies within the domain of politics.

5. A variety of different organizational arrangements can be used to provide different public goods and services. Such organizations can be coordinated through various multi-organizational arrangements including trading and contracting to mutual advantage, competitive rivalry, adjudication, as well as the power of command in limited hierarchies.

6. Perfection in the hierarchical ordering of a professionally trained public service accountable to a *single* center of power will reduce the capability of a large administrative system to respond to diverse preferences among citizens for many different public goods and services and cope with diverse environmental conditions.

7. Perfection in hierarchical organization accountable to a *single* center of power will *not* maximize efficiency as measured by least-cost expended in time, effort, and resources.

8. Fragmentation of authority among diverse decision centers with multiple veto capabilities within any one jurisdiction and the development of multiple, overlapping jurisdictions of widely different scales are necessary conditions for maintaining a stable political order which can advance human welfare under rapidly changing conditions.

A theory of democratic administration does not preclude a theory of bureaucratic administration. But acceptance of a theory of democratic administration does imply a rejection of the assertion that a theory of bureaucratic administration is the only theory of good administration for all governments alike. The existence of two theories of public administration still poses a serious problem for American students and practitioners of public administration. What theory and mode of analysis is appropriate to the practice of American public administration?[6]

What happens when a highly polycentric system of democratic administration is modified and changed to conform to the precepts of a monocentric system of bureaucratic administration? Is there a possibility that such alterations and reforms will exceed the limits for maintaining an enforceable system of constitutional rule? Are we prepared to pay that price? Will there be a threshold beyond which the price of peace is one of servitude in a bureaucratic despotism? It is some of these questions that have led me to entertain the outlandish hypothesis which I introduced in the first lecture: Dare we contemplate the possibility that the contemporary malaise in American society may have been derived, in part, from the teachings of public administration? Have our reform efforts to eliminate fragmentation of authority and overlapping jurisdictions so altered the basic structure of American government that many of its benefits have been eliminated as well? If we continue to use one theory of political design to reform a system based with another theory of design, may we confront a vicious circle where the more we do the worse off we become? Without an appropriate theory of political organization, we shall be unable to discern the causes of our misery and we shall suffer ills of which we are ignorant. (Tocqueville, 1835:I, 239–240.)

The Use of Different Approaches to Policy Analysis

In continuing our inquiry into these different approaches to the study of public administration, I propose that we begin to explore the implications that each will have for the solution to some contemporary problems confronting the American people. A choice of paradigm can be expected to influence our diagnosis of sources of institutional weaknesses which give rise to social pathologies. Proposals for reform will also be derived from the choice of paradigm. Once we become more fully aware of the significance attached to a choice of paradigm, we can become more critical of our own work as scholars and of the implication that our work has for the practice of public administration in a democratic society. The use of different paradigms may indeed lead to alternative designs for alternative futures.

POLICY ANALYSIS OF INSTITUTIONAL ARRANGEMENTS IN URBAN AREAS

The power and persistence of the Wilsonian paradigm is reflected in its continued use as a basis for policy analysis and for proposals of institutional reform. The prestigious Committee for Economic Development, for example, drew upon that paradigm in preparing its report on *Modernizing Local Government* (1966). Its more recent report on *Reshaping Government in Metropolitan Areas* (1970) adheres less rigorously to that paradigm but con-tinues to use the language of the traditional paradigm

The diagnostic assessment of the conditions of institutional weakness and institutional failure contained in the first CED report (1966) are based upon the following findings:

1. Very few of the local units (of government) are large enough—in population, area, or taxable resources—to apply modern methods in solving current and future problems. Even the largest cities find major problems insoluble because of the limits on geographic areas, their taxable resources, or their legal powers.
2. Overlapping layers of local government—municipalities and townships within counties, and independent school districts within them—are a source of weakness. . . .This (overlapping) impairs overall local

[114]

freedom to deal with vital public affairs; the whole becomes less than the sum of its parts.

3. Popular control over government is ineffective and sporadic, and public interest in local politics is not high-.... Confusion from the many layered system, profusion of elective offices without policy significance, and increasing mobility of the population all contribute to disinterest.

4. Policy-making mechanisms in many units are notably weak. The national government (by contrast) has strong executive leadership, supported by competent staff in formulating plans that are then subject to review and modification by a representative legislative body....

5. Antiquated administrative organizations hamper most local governments. Lack of a single executive either elective or appointive is a common fault. Functional fragmentation obscures lines of authority.... The quality of administration suffers accordingly. (CED, 1966: 11–12.)

This analysis stresses the existence of numerous units of government, overlapping jurisdictions, and fragmentation of authority to infer that such events are causally linked to problems of institutional failure in urban communities. A monocentric political system with a hierarchically ordered administrative structure accountable to a single chief executive is used as a yardstick for ascertaining the preferred solution. The principal recommendation included in the CED report for *Modernizing Local Government* includes the following:

1. The number of local governments in the United States, now about 80,000, should be reduced by at least 80 percent.

2. The number of overlapping layers of local government found in most states should be sharply curtailed.

3. Popular elections should be confined to members of

the policy making body, and to the chief executive in those governments where the "strong mayor" form is preferred to the "council-manager" plan.

4. Each unit should have a single chief executive, either elected by the people or appointed by the local legislative body, with all administrative agencies and personnel fully responsible to him; election of department heads should be halted. (CED, 1966:17.)

While focusing on the costs of overlap and complexity, the CED report completely discounts *any* costs associated with institutional weakness and institutional failure in large-scale public bureaucracies. No recognition is given to the substantial literature in organization theory on the problem of goal displacement and bureaucratic dysfunctions. The concept of bureaucracy as an ideal-type solution pervades the CED analysis.

Citizens in a democratic society will run a very substantial risk if they are asked to stake their future upon ideal-type formulations. Anyone offering perpetual-motion machines for sale would be exposed to a potential charge of fraud. Perhaps it is a reflection upon the contemporary state of political science that a distinguished group of businessmen advised by a distinguished group of political scientists can recommend that eighty percent of the units of local government should be eliminated without making any efforts to assess the opportunity costs inherent in such a solution. Sixty thousand units of local government represent a major investment in decision-making facilities among the American people. Their elimination would be destructive of the basic infrastructure of American democratic administration. Can we afford to pay that price?

And what would we be buying at the costs of eliminating most of the infrastructure of American democratic administration? Tullock's analysis of institutional failure in large-scale bureaucracies would suggest that we would be buying increasing measures of corruption associated with bureaucratic free enterprise. The prevalence of corruption in big-city police forces is data that can hardly be ignored. Big-city police departments are systematically failing to respond to demands for public security. Employment of private guards and private security forces is assuming a substantial magnitude.[7] Such expenditures clearly indicate that people are willing to pay for public services which police departments fail to render.

Among the less prosperous segments of the population in big cities, we observe a similar increase in demand for public security which is being met by the organization of neighborhood patrols and escort services through various forms of neighborhood improvement associations, churches, and other voluntary associations. In addition, many of the urban gangs function essentially as mutual protection societies. Some of these organizations are evolving into the equivalent of "soldier societies" capable of protecting their own domain or "turf" and of levying sufficient tribute to maintain viable organizations.

Aggressive rivalry between organized police and organized "soldier societies" is developing to a point where covert warfare is manifest by sporadic outbreaks of overt violence. The modern police tactic of "aggressive patrol" conducted by special task forces is no less than a military strategy to impose collective sanctions upon urban neighborhoods. (Graham, 1968.) The peace of democratic communities depends upon the good will and helping hand of the individuals who comprise those communities. (Jacobs, 1968.) Law and order maintained by the commanding power of an alien force is in fundamental violation of the most basic precepts of democratic administration.

Claims of efficiency in large-scale bureaucratic organizations can be supported only so long as ideal performance is postulated for a bureaucratic machine. Much of the literature in public administration pervasively ignores

[117]

the problem of size even though the principle of span of control implies a radical constraint upon organizational size. The notion that "there is little hard economic evidence of what *the* optimal size should be" (CED, 1970:20. My emphasis.) is valid only so long as *a single optimum* is presumed. The theory of externalities, common properties, and public goods would postulate the criterion that the domain of a public agency should coincide with boundaries of the appropriate field of effects so that substantial interdependencies are internalized within the jurisdiction of an appropriate agency. (Ostrom, Tiebout and Warren, 1961; Olson, 1969.) Optimal size will vary with the boundary conditions of *different* fields of effects inherent in the provision of *different* public goods and services. Under these conditions, optimality can be attained only by reference to multiple agencies with overlapping jurisdictions. (Tullock, 1969.)

Economists do not anticipate that a single optimum size will exist for the different types of services produced for *any one* industry. Instead, economic provision of the services rendered by a particular industry will require a complex of agencies of many different sizes. A firm capable of producing automobiles at the lowest marginal cost will vary in size from a firm capable of repairing automobiles at the lowest marginal cost. Similarly we would expect that the size of a police agency capable of facilitating optimal movement of automobile traffic through a metropolitan area will be different from a police agency capable of optimally satisfying the demands of neighborhood residents for public security in neighborhood streets. (E. Ostrom and Whitaker, 1971a and 1971b.)

Economists would expect different types of economic activities to reflect different economies of scale. Some services will be produced more efficiently by large-scale enterprises. The converse is also true: some services will

[118]

be produced more efficiently by small-scale enterprises. Where capital costs in plants or physical facilities are proportionately large, economies of scale will accrue if those costs can be spread over a large number of users. Conversely, where labor costs or personnel services comprise a large proportion of the budget in the provision of a public service, economies of scale will be exhausted by smaller-sized organizations. If a public agency is user-oriented in providing a service to satisfy the diverse interests of individuals and members of households, such agencies will be subject to very limited economies of scale. Neighborhood government and community control would be appropriate mechanisms to use in the provision of some public goods and services within big cities. (Altschuler, 1970; Kotler, 1969.)

Werner Hirsch (1964 and 1968), in reviewing different studies of economies of scale among public sector agencies, indicates that the opportunities for improvements in efficiency through increased size will have been exhausted for many services in communities that reach a size of 50–150,000 population. Exceptions to this conclusion apply to capital-intensive utility services such as water supply, transportation, and sewage disposal. Even then, factors relative to the resource base may lead to radical variations in economies of scale.

Urban populations of 50–150,000 are small in size when compared to the major metropolitan areas of the United States. The diseconomies of scale associated with large-scale organization of many urban services has led George Stigler to conclude:

> If we give each governmental activity to the smallest governmental unit which can efficiently perform it, there will be a vast resurgence and revitalization of local government in America. A vast reservoir of ability and imagination can be found in the increasing leisure time of the population, and both public functions and private citizens would benefit

from the increased participation of citizens in political life. An eminent and powerful structure of local government is a basic ingredient of a society which seeks to give the individual the fullest possible freedom and responsibility. (Stigler, 1962:146.)

Serious problems of institutional failure would occur if *only* small units of government were relied upon to perform functions of local government. The problem of "balkanization" in local government can, however, be resolved by an appropriate overlapping of local governmental jurisdictions so that significant interdependencies of a regional character can be handled by regional authorities. Tullock has suggested that the Buchanan and Tullock cost calculus is applicable to a choice of the optimum amount of overlap in a highly federalized political system. (Tullock, 1969.) Stigler's solution is viable only if advantage can be taken of the presence of overlapping jurisdictions in metropolitan areas.

The CED's most recent report on *Reshaping Government in Metropolitan Areas* (1970) reflects a major shift in emphasis by recognizing some variations in scale economies. A two-level arrangement is called for with a general unit of government for each metropolitan area and numerous community districts within each metropolitan area. This report indicates a willingness to sacrifice "neatness and symmetry" for greater "effectiveness and responsiveness." (CED, 1970:19.) A case is made for centralization and decentralization as accruing concurrently in a two-level structure. The report calls for "a genuine sharing of power over functions" without explicitly recognizing that such a condition *necessarily* requires fragmentation of authority and overlapping jurisdictions. (CED, 1970:17, 19–20.) The report is still furbished in the usual phrases about a "fragmented system of government," and "overlapping local units" as

[120]

forming "a confusing maze." (CED, 1970:10.) The present system is reported to work better for suburbanites than for the residents of central cities without deriving any conclusion that institutional failure may accrue from *the absence of overlapping jurisdictions and fragmented authority within central cities.*

More than a shift of emphasis is called for in our analysis of urban problems. Streets can no longer be kept clean in many areas of the great City of New York. School administrators can no longer cope with cockroaches in the City of Los Angeles. *(Los Angeles Times,* August 13, 1971.) The technologies have long existed for cleaning streets and controlling cockroaches; but modern, professional administrators are somehow unable to mobilize the means to perform simple but essential tasks at appropriate times and places. When the *possible* becomes *impossible,* we have reason to believe that problems of institutional failure have reached massive proportions.

Perhaps we should begin to explore some of the *opportunities* which exist among overlapping jurisdictions in metropolitan areas. (Tiebout, 1956; Ostrom, Tiebout and Warren, 1961; Warren, 1964; Warren, 1966; Bish, 1971.) In southern California, for example, many cities are taking *advantage* of overlapping jurisdictions by contracting for the provision of different types of public goods and services. Under this arrangement a municipality may function as a buyers' cooperative where its chief administrative officer serves as a purchasing agent to search out the most favorable alternative for procuring a public service. If citizens have complaints about services rendered, the chief administrative officer will represent their interest in demanding performance from the vendor. The vendor must strive to meet community demands or be confronted with the possibility that the city as a buyers' cooperative will contract with another vendor or establish its own services.

Competitive rivalry among diverse public agencies operating within a municipal-services industry composed of jurisdictions capable of tending to diverse communities of interest may offer an alternative approach to the realization of efficiency in government. The contemporary political economists in approaching a choice of institutional arrangements for the organization of government in metropolitan areas would attempt to examine different alternative possibilities and recommend that alternative which would render individuals the best service for their money. The recommended solution based upon the criterion of efficiency is the alternative that would give individuals the greatest net advantage. Perhaps we need to be more attuned to the principle of relative advantage in our policy analyses than to the logic of ideal forms.

Policy Analysis of the Administration of National Affairs

Similar paradigmatic problems exist in the analysis of public policy relative to the conduct of national public affairs. Since the formulation of Luther Gulick's anomalous orthodoxy in preparing the report for the President's Committee on Administrative Management, the thrust of policy analysis in national affairs has focused largely upon strengthening the President as chief executive. Herbert Emmerich in his Alabama lectures on Federal reorganization, for example, defines reorganization as

> . . . a change in the size, distribution, and nature of executive functions, or their staffing and financing and particularly when these changes measurably affect the ability of the head of the executive branch—the President—to supervise and direct the manner in which these functions are exercised. (Emmerich, 1950:7.)

[122]

For Emmerich, reorganization "envisions goals that necessarily transcend the objectives of efficiency and economy. . . ." (Emmerich, 1950:8.) These goals relate to the strengthening of the office of the President: "The Presidency is the focal point of any study of reorganization." (Emmerich, 1950:7.)

James L. Sundquist of the Brookings Institution follows in this tradition to suggest that Federal coordination of *community assistance programs* necessarily depends upon Presidential direction:

> The facts of bureaucratic life are that no cabinet department has ever been able to act effectively, for long, as a central coordinator of other departments of equal rank that are its competitors for authority and funds. Nor does coordination spring readily from the mutual adjustment of Cabinet level equals within the federal hierarchy. *It must be induced, overseen, managed, and directed from the supra-Cabinet level— in other words from the Executive Office of the President, where the authority exists to identify problems that need settlement, expedite discussion, referee disputes, make binding decisions, and issue orders.* Voluntary bargaining among Cabinet departments of equal rank is no substitute for a decision-making structure led by a presidential staff officer who carries the authority and the governmentwide perspective of the President. (Sundquist, 1969: 244–245. My emphasis.)

Sundquist, like so many other policy analysts, gives no consideration to the costs associated with the addition of new coordinating and directing structures in the Executive Offices of the President. Sundquist fails to identify how coordinating agencies, in the absence of operating responsibilities, are to identify problems needing settlement, expedite discussions, referee disputes, and make binding decisions in *community assistance programs* from the Executive Offices of the President unless those who are elected to the Presidency and those who are appointed to the Executive Offices are presumed to be both omniscient and omnicompetent.

Presumptions of omniscience and omnicompetence cannot hold in the design of national institutional arrangements any more than presumptions of frictionless motion can hold in applied mechanics. Reliance upon such presumptions will generate a rhetoric based upon concepts which are inappropriate to the resolution of policy problems. The community assistance programs were generated in President Johnson's rhetorical "War on Poverty." Some problems may be tractable to a massive mobilization for a frontal onslaught; but human poverty is not one of those problems. The notion that a commander in chief will mobilize an integrated and comprehensive effort by *all* agencies of government in *attacking* the multitudinous causes of poverty while simultaneously sustaining numerous other wars, campaigns, and crusades may be politically expedient rhetoric but it will *not* solve the problems of poverty, eliminate pollution, stop crimes in the streets, or ameliorate the urban crisis. Expenditure of massive amounts of public funds on the assumption that spending money will solve *any* problem is also destined to failure.

Once a President becomes rhetorically committed to a "War on Poverty" or a "War on Crime" we might reasonably infer that subordinates will facilitate the transmission of favorable information and deter the transmission of unfavorable information. Thus, the hierarchy of command in the Executive Offices of the President will induce a multiplier effect in generating and transmitting misinformation. The larger the executive establishment in the Executive Offices becomes, the less accessible the President will be to those outside the Executive Offices including members of Congress, officials in the various departments and bureaus of the national government, and persons outside the formal structure of the national government. The more insulated the President becomes, the

[124]

more Presidential decision making will exhibit error proneness.

Measures taken to solve problems by the rhetoric of warfare and the politics of crisis will exacerbate many problems rather than alleviate them. Performance will radically diverge from expectations; and the illusion of perpetual crisis will permeate public affairs. If the illusion gives way to skepticism, then the credibility gap will become an institutionalized feature of American public life. Warfare rhetoric, crisis politics, and credibility gaps are unfortunate ingredients in the public life of people living in a potentially dangerous world. The rhetoric of crisis, like the cry of "wolf," will not be heeded if frequently used in inappropriate circumstances.

Reiterating the prescription for strengthening Presidential prerogative as a major remedy for dealing with community assistance programs, rural development activities, the quality of the environment, poverty, law and order, and urban affairs comes close to articulating a slogan of "All Power to the President." If all such recommendations were to be implemented, what consequences would we predict for the future of American democracy?

It is the exigencies of national defense that peculiarly require a system of one-man rule inherent in the prerogatives of commander in chief—not the exigencies of community assistance programs, rural development, poverty, or the public security of neighborhood streets. The advantage of surprise in a military attack requires utmost speed and dispatch in mobilizing defenses against an attack. Speed and dispatch can indeed be facilitated by reducing the number of decision makers to a minimum of one. But a decision rule of one also gives strategic opportunities for that one decision maker to pursue preemptive strategies that foreclose due deliberation regarding the opportunity costs inherent in public choices. The rhetoric of supreme sacrifice—of sustaining action "at all cost"

[125]

or "at any price"—is the mark of preemptive leadership. Tragedies ensue when *supreme sacrifices* are exacted for trivial interests or misconceived objectives.

The office of President is an *essential element* in the American constitutional system. There are circumstances where decision costs must be minimized and critical actions must be taken with speed and dispatch. Such circumstances can at most involve a small number of decisions. A President cannot proceed with equal speed and dispatch in treating all the problems of some 200 million people. An overloaded President with a large executive establishment exercising control from the Executive Offices of the President can become a critical source of institutional failure in the American system of government. Institutional failure in the American Presidency will be marked by an increasing proneness to error and to dilettantism. Using the rhetoric of warfare and of crisis politics to dabble with such difficult and persistent problems as human poverty can only engender profound skepticism and cynicism regarding the efficacy of American public administration.

If we are concerned about human poverty, community assistance programs, rural development, the public security of neighborhood streets, and the quality of the environment, should we proceed on an assumption that these are all *national problems* requiring *national solutions* which can only be solved by Presidential intervention? Or should we proceed on the assumption that these problems are but names for a multitude of difficulties confronting individual human beings as they pursue their relative advantage in dealing with one another? If we were to proceed on the latter assumption, we might use a science of association to diagnose the existing allocation of decision-making capabilities to ascertain *why* the prevailing structures or forms of human association generate the consequences they do. We might then be in a position to propose structural modifications for evoking different consequences.

Instead of appealing to Presidential prerogative as a solution to all problems, we might, for example, inquire into the structural conditions of a culture of poverty. Perhaps we might begin by examining the structure of the rent bargain to determine whether the prevailing structure of relationships among tenants and landlords tends to evoke consequences analogous to the tragedy of the commons. Is the dilapidated housing of ghetto communities a manifestation of negative-sum games inextricably working themselves out in human tragedies? (Davis and Whinston, 1961.)

If so, are there ways that the rent bargain might be restructured so that landlords and tenants could act jointly to realize a mutual advantage from the opportunities available to them? How would relationships between landlords and tenants be modified if a right to collective bargaining were extended to tenants? Would tenants bargain on behalf of their common interest to control rats, cockroaches, and other pests? Would they seek improvements in joint facilities such as laundries and waste disposal facilities? Would they seek better building maintenance? Would they seek to improve their relationships as neighbors?

Other alternatives for modifying the rent bargain might also be considered. Will the condominium work for the poor as well as for the rich? What would happen if tenants in an apartment building were allowed to incorporate as a public corporation and exercise the power of eminent domain to acquire ownership of the building they occupy?[8] Would tenant unions and tenant corporations provide individuals with a more effective instrumentality for articulating demands regarding the delivery of better-quality public services? Can we imagine modifications in the rent bargain where tenants would have an incentive to seek improvements in the quality of their neighborhood community? Would organized tenants demand cleaner streets? Would they demand greater public security in neighborhood streets? Would modifications in the rent bargain improve the quality of the urban environment and strengthen the possibility for neighborhood government and community control within the big city?

If we approach the problems of poverty and crime in the street from a science of association inherent in a theory of democratic administration, we would search for solutions which will minimize a strict subordination in command structures. We would avoid the rhetoric of warfare in mobilizing *all* resources of the nation for a *comprehensive attack* upon either poverty or crime as *national* problems. Instead, we would be concerned with allocating decision-making capabilities so that discretion can be exercised to take mutual advantage of joint opportunities available to the persons involved.

Democratic administration depends upon avoiding the presumptions of monopoly power in the conduct both of public policy analysis and of public affairs. Using Max Weber's criteria of democratic administration, policy analysts in that tradition would be concerned with how to enhance citizen participation in community development, social welfare, and public order. Voluntary action by citizens in providing for the common welfare of fellow citizens has a place in democratic societies which can never be fully replaced by paid functionaries and mass mobilization campaigns. Policy analysts in the tradition of democratic administration would show a preference for small-scale enterprises over large-scale enterprises where such scales are appropriate to the domain of particular public goods and services. They would also be concerned to proportion costs to benefits so that individuals can have a sense of reality about the opportunity costs

[128]

inherent in collective action. They would seek to establish decision structures which will require public officials to maintain a due dependence upon their constituents and facilitate the participation of those constituents and their representatives in the taking of important decisions. Democratic administration depends upon elections, representation, and open deliberation in common councils for reaching collective decisions.

The task in fashioning a system of democratic administration is how to restrict the power of command to a minimum and substitute structures of economic, political, and judicial control rather than rely upon a single over-reaching bureaucracy to coordinate all human efforts. Such controls should be devised so that public servants as public entrepreneurs are exposed to the necessity of taking account of an appropriate cost calculus, the preferences of their constituents, and the legal constraints of constitutional and public laws that bear upon the organization and conduct of collective enterprises. Such controls can sustain viable enterprises capable of substantial efficiency where public entrepreneurs are oriented toward serving their constituents rather than becoming political masters.

In the administration of national affairs, Presidential prerogative is of critical importance for dealing with the exigencies of warfare. However, the exigencies of warfare will, in the long run, be destructive of constitutional rule in a democratic society.

Hamilton once observed that:

Safety from external danger is the most powerful director of national conduct. Even the ardent love of liberty will, after a time, give way to its dictates. The violent destruction of life and property incident to war, the continual effort and alarm attendant on a state of continual danger, will compel nations the most attached to liberty to resort for repose and security in institutions which have the tendency to destroy

[129]

their civil and political rights. To be more safe, they at length will become willing to run the risk of being less free. *(Federalist* 8.)

Hamilton also recognized that the exigencies of war will lead people "to strengthen the executive arm of government, in doing which their constitutions would acquire a progressive direction toward monarchy. It is the nature of war to increase the executive at the expense of the legislative power." *(Federalist* 8.)

The American solution of 1787 was an effort to fashion a political solution where all our political experiments would be predicated upon the capacity of mankind for self-government. *(Federalist* 39.) The search for political solutions among communities of people sharing interdependent interests in the collective security of nations is an alternative to allowing the logic of warfare—of accident and force—to dominate the constitution of human societies. The task of constraining Presidential prerogative depends upon the constitution of diverse international communities capable of tending to limited problems of common concern. The future of the free world depends upon more overlapping jurisdictions and fragmentation of authority, not less.

Conclusion

Thus, I would conclude that Hobbes was right in fashioning a constitution appropriate to a garrison state capable of functioning with reasonable effectiveness in a world plagued by recurrent warfare. I would also contend that Hamilton and Madison were right in presuming that societies of men are capable of establishing good government by reflection and choice where a system of constitutional rule can be enforced in a political system characterized by substantial fragmentation of authority and overlapping jurisdictions. Such a constitutional system is capable of maintaining democratic administration as a general form of public administration which stands in contradistinction to bureaucratic administration.

If I am correct, practitioners and students of public administration will need to rethink both the theory and practice of their science of administration. The practitioner of American public administration, if he is to contribute to the viability of a democratic society, must be prepared to advance and serve the interests of the individual persons who form his relevant public.[9] His service is to individual persons as users or consumers of public goods and services and not to political masters. He respects the authority of governmental officials who help define and limit the scope of public endeavors. He sustains a reasoned contention on behalf of interests which he perceives to be essential. He uses his knowledge to serve others; and in the course of doing so, he and others join in mutual efforts to enhance their common weal.[10] The value of the knowledge that he professes and uses as tools of analysis, and as guides for action, is measured by its usefulness for enhancing the welfare of discrete human beings.

The public servant in a democratic society is not a neutral and obedient servant to his master's command. He will refuse to obey unlawful efforts to exploit the common wealth or to use the coercive capabilities of the state to impair the rights of persons, but he will use reason and peaceful persuasion in taking such stands. Each public servant in the American system of democratic administration bears first the burden of being a citizen in a constitutional republic; and citizenship in a constitutional republic depends upon a willingness to bear the costs for enforcing the rules of constitutional law against those who exercise the prerogatives of government.

Fashioning the architecture for a system of democratic administration will require different concepts and different solutions from those which can be derived from Wilson, Goodnow, Willoughby, White, and Gulick. Instead, a new theory of democratic administration will have to be fashioned from the works of Hamilton, Madison, Tocqueville, Dewey, Lindblom, Buchanan, Tullock, Olson, Niskanen, and many others. The theory of externalities, common properties, and public goods, the logic of collective action and public enterprise, the concepts of public-service industries, and fiscal federalism will have prominent places in that theory. Attention will shift from a preoccupation with *the* organization to concerns with the opportunities that individuals can pursue in a multi-organizational environment. Policy analysis will focus upon problems of institutional weakness and institutional failure inherent in any organizational structure or institutional arrangement. Policy recommendations will be presented with greater emphasis upon the opportunity costs inherent in different organizational arrangements.

A democratic theory of administration will not be preoccupied with simplicity, neatness, and symmetry but with diversity, variety, and responsiveness to the preferences of constituents. A system of democratic administration depends upon an ordered complexity in social relationships. In such a system, it is the task of scholars to formulate a science of association which will enable communities of people to fashion organizational arrangements which will put individual self-interest to proper use as a rule for action in advancing human welfare. A new political science is needed for a new world if the human potentials of democratic societies are to be realized through a system of democratic administration. Success depends upon a knowledge of both the *capabilities* and *limitations* of diverse organizational forms which can be used to minimize the power of command and yield services to enhance the welfare of people.

A system of democratic administration based upon structures of overlapping jurisdictions and fragmented authority can indeed provide a "historical starting point" for a new course of human development. As Jean-Francois Revel has observed:

> The revolution of the twentieth century will take place in the United States. It is only there that it can happen. And it has already begun. Whether or not that revolution spreads to the rest of the world depends on whether or not it succeeds first in America. (Revel, 1971:1.)

The success of this new American revolution depends, in part, upon whether or not American students and practitioners of public administration are prepared to reject Wilson's theses and fashion a new theory of democratic administration appropriate to the organization of diverse public enterprises in democratic societies. The new theory needs to return to the revolutionary thrust inherent in the American experiment. (Arendt, 1963.) The Wilsonian theory of administration was no less than a counter-revolutionary doctrine. Perhaps the American experiment—predicated upon the capacity of mankind for self-government—has only begun to realize its potential.

Watergate and the Constitutional Crisis of the 1970's

IN THE CONCLUDING LECTURE, I WARNED OF THE PROBLEMS that can arise when one theory of organization is used to make alterations in governmental structures based upon a different theory of organization.

An appropriate theory of design is necessary both to understand how a system will work and how modifications or changes in a system will affect its performance. To use one theory of design to evaluate the characteristics of a system based upon a different theory of design can lead to profound misunderstandings. To use one theory of design to reform a system based upon a different theory of design may produce many unanticipated and costly consequences. (*Supra:* 102.)

The basic conflicts over contending theories which evoke intellectual crises among communities of scholars can also be the source of political and constitutional crises when those theories are used in organizing human actions.[1]

Watergate: A Constitutional Crisis Over Executive Authority

The "Watergate" affair was initially revealed as an episode in partisan politics when several Republican partisans were arrested for unlawful entry into the headquarters of the Democratic National Committee. Subsequent investigations have provided substantial evidence that the arrests at Watergate were only a minor episode in the abuse of executive authority. Each of the individuals arrested had had associations with the Special Investigations Unit in the Executive Offices of the President or with the Central Intelligence Agency. Other members of the White House staff have also been indicted for charges associated with burglarizing the offices of a psychiatrist to procure information about a former government employee.

Testimony in the Watergate hearings indicates that large sums of cash, not subject to public accounting, have been available to top White House personnel. A former police officer, employed through a private law firm, was used to conduct investigations for the staff of the Domestic Council. "Enemy" lists were formulated to include persons not in favor at the White House. Strong circumstantial evidence suggests that Federal tax audits and criminal justice procedures have been used to harass persons actively opposed to the administration. Thin threads of evidence appear to indicate that killings without due process of law have been practiced against Black Panthers.

The Vice-President has been convicted of a felony associated with the unlawful receipt and use of funds paid for bribery. Two former cabinet officers are under indictment for charges associated with irregular payments of funds. In the midst of these irregularities the President claims executive immunity for withholding evidence pertinent to proceedings in grand juries, trial courts, and Congressional committees. Presidential prerogative is being asserted to limit the scope of criminal investigations in relation to high officials in the Executive Offices of the President. Whether a President may lawfully use the cloak of his office to impede such proceedings is becoming a critical constitutional issue. A constitutional crisis of major proportions has been provoked over issues involving executive authority.

The current constitutional crisis can be viewed as the consequence of a long series of efforts to "strengthen" the Executive[2] and to center all control over Federal administration in the Executive Offices of the President. These efforts reflect the central tenet of American scholarship in public administration: unity of command. The Brownlow Committee in the Roosevelt Administration formulated the basic design. The recommendations have been reiterated by the Hoover Commissions, the recent Ash Council, and countless other reorganization efforts. Substantial success has been attained in these efforts to strengthen the Executive.

Following the work of the Brownlow Committee and the Hoover Commissions, Congress in the Administrative Reorganization Acts of 1939 and 1949 extended authority to the President to promulgate reorganization plans that would have the force of law, subject to a legislative veto within a sixty-day period. By these Acts, Congress conveyed substantial law-making authority upon the President to reallocate executive authority for the conduct of the Federal government. On the basis of this authority, President Nixon submitted, on March 12, 1970, "Reorganization Plan No. 2 of 1970," to go into effect on July 1 of that year in the absence of adverse legislative action. Congress did not act. This reorganization plan contains much of the essential structure for creating a legally omnipotent Executive.

The presidential message transmitting Reorganization Plan No. 2 states the basic rationale for that reorganization effort. Two basic functions of government are identified as centering in the Office of the President. These are "policy determination" and "executive management." (*U.S. Codes, Congressional and Administrative Laws* 91st Cong. 2 Sess., 1970, Vol. III: 6316. Hereafter cited as

U.S. Codes.) These two functions, according to the message, involve questions of "(1) what Government should do and (2) how it goes about doing it." (*U.S. Codes,* ibid.) The plan creates a new entity to perform each function. The Domestic Council is created to assist the President in deciding "what Government should do," and the Office of Management and Budget (OMB) is created to assist the President in determining "*how* we do it and *how* well we do it." (*U.S. Codes,* ibid.)

The legal architecture inherent in Reorganization Plan No. 2 is a basic conveyance of authority. All functions vested by law in the Bureau of the Budget or in the Director of the Bureau of the Budget were transferred to the President. The old Bureau of the Budget was designated as the Office of Management and Budget. The Director of OMB was assigned responsibility to perform "such functions as the President may from time to time delegate and assign thereto." (*U.S. Codes,* ibid., p. 6320.) The President is the effective *director* of OMB; the appointed Director is his administrative assistant.

The Domestic Council, as the body to decide "what Government should do," is to be composed of the President, the Vice-President, several cabinet officers, and such other offices of the executive branch as the President may direct. The council is to perform "such functions as the President may from time to time delegate and assign thereto." (*U.S. Codes,* ibid., p. 6321.) An assistant to the President designated by the President to serve as Executive Director of the Domestic Council is to direct the council's staff in the performance of "such functions as the President may from time to time direct." (*U.S. Codes,* ibid.) Again the legal structure of the Domestic Council implies that decisions about "what Government should do" are to be taken at the direction of the President.

Woodrow Wilson, by contrast, presumed that Congress had the prerogative to decide "what shall be done" and that the President "is plainly bound in duty to render un-questioning obedience to Congress." (Wilson, 1885:181.) But who is to enforce that duty if the President commands the entire executive establishment?

The accompanying message indicates that OMB will perform management functions beyond those previously exercised by the Bureau of the Budget. OMB was assigned responsibility for executive personnel in policy positions and in the top ranks of the civil service. Control over top-level executive personnel is a new OMB management tool. In addition, OMB is to be responsible for "Washington-based coordinators" who will coordinate interagency relationships at operating levels "throughout the country." (*U.S. Codes,* ibid., p. 6318.) Presumably, these "Washington-based coordinators" are to assist in coordinating intergovernmental relationships among state and local governments as well.

Reference is also made to the improvement of govern-ment organization and the development of new informa-tion and management systems as being major functions of OMB. The message anticipates that "resistance to organizational change is one of the chief obstacles to effec-tive government" and implies that such resistance needs to be overcome in order to ensure that "organization keeps abreast of program needs." (*U.S. Codes,* ibid.)

A New Administrative State?

Reorganization Plan No. 2 presumes that the President as Chief Executive has ultimate authority over the entire executive establishment. Decisions about *what* govern-ment should do and *how* it is done are within his preroga-tive. If basic authority to exercise a unified command over the federal executive establishment is to reside in the President, several implications follow about the legal force of presidential instructions, channels for command over the executive establishment, and mechanisms for enforcing compliance.

PRESIDENTIAL INSTRUCTIONS AS EFFECTIVE LAW?

The most general provision of the U.S. Constitution, defining the authority of the President as Chief Executive, is contained in the clause "... he shall take care that the laws be faithfully executed." (Article II, Sec. 3.) The emphasis here is upon the enforcement or execution of law. The law-making functions of government are identified with Congress within the constraints provided by the more general law laid down in the Constitution itself. A separate and independent judiciary was established to determine conflicts and render judgment in controversies over the application of law.

Where the functions of policy determination and executive management are fully integrated in a unified command structure exercised in the Office of President, discretion for determining the legal force that will be given to public law resides with the President. The attorney general is his subordinate as are all employees within the Justic Department and other agencies of the Federal government. Subordinate employees are subject to dismissal for failure to defer to presidential prerogative. Prosecutors who proceed too diligently in matters of potential embarrassment to the President are subject to dismissal. In his dismissal of Archibald Cox as special prosecutor, President Nixon has, for example, observed in a letter to the acting attorney general:

In his press conference today ... Cox made it apparent that he will not comply with the instructions I issued to him, through Attorney General Richardson, yesterday. Clearly the government of the United States cannot function if

[139]

employees of the executive branch are free to ignore in this fashion the instructions of the President. Accordingly, in your capacity as acting attorney general, I direct you to discharge Mr. Cox immediately. (*Sunday Herald-Times*, Bloomington, Ind., Oct. 21, 1973, p. 1.)

In this case presidential determination of policy overrides considerations of whether Prosecutor Cox was lawfully and diligently discharging his responsibility to proceed with criminal investigations of possible felonies committed by members and former members of the President's White House staff. If the grounds for dismissal are failure to conform to presidential instruction and not failure to discharge his legal responsibilities under law, then Cox's dismissal implies that presidential instructions prevail over other provisions of law. Issues regarding presidential impoundment of funds appropriated by Congress and presidential actions to dismantle the Office of Economic Opportunity raise similar questions about the intervening force of presidential instructions as effective law.

No presumption exists that presidential instructions will be publicized as the public acts of a public authority. Instead, presidential instructions can be secret instructions protected by executive immunity. The internal affairs of an omnipotent executive are always cloaked in a passion for anonymity.[3]

Thomas Hobbes long ago recognized that "covenants without the sword are but words. . . . " (Hobbes, 1651: 109.) The force of law depends critically upon executive discretion and executive action. Enforcement is an essential condition of effective law. As responsibility for "policy determination" and "executive management" over the federal administrative establishment are centralized in the Office of President, the meaning of statutory law will turn increasingly on presidential instruction. Policy decisions taken by reference to statutory provisions can be overridden by presidential instruction. Under such circumstances presidential instructions become effective law.

When presidential instructions become effective law, enactments by Congress will then serve only as general statements of principle or of purpose. In Hobbes' terms, Acts of Congress would then be mere "words." Legislation will become positive morality, in John Austin's language, not positive law. (Austin, 1832.) When legislation becomes positive morality, not positive law, then Congress will be relegated to the performance of ceremonial functions in proclaiming moral platitudes about public life.

Whether Presidential instructions become effective law will turn critically upon the decisions rendered by the judiciary in acting upon proceedings initiated by citizens and by nonfederal officials. The legal architecture for the new administrative state, thus, has a serious flaw. To correct that flaw, Administrative Reorganization Plan No. 2 will need to be supplemented by a new reorganization plan creating a Council of State to take its place alongside the Domestic Council in the Executive Offices of the President. The French *Conseil d'Etat* provides the approximate model. The Council of State would be composed of high officials in the executive branch presided over by the attorney general as the President's chief legal officer. The function of the council and its staff would be to consider grievances and adjudicate conflicts involving the claims of citizens in relation to the exercise of executive discretion. Determinations of the Council of State would be final in all matters of executive discretion. Presidential instructions would become effective law and precedent would be abandoned as a principle for construing law. The regular courts would be relieved of an onerous burden of work. Public law would become administrative law. Constitutional law would no longer exist.

A New Executive Service?

Alexis de Tocqueville, in his study of the *ancien regime,* reports how the management of internal affairs in France was organized through a single official—a controller-general—who exercised authority through Paris-based coordinators, called intendants, who assumed responsibility for coordinating interagency relationships throughout France. Tocqueville quotes the following observation made by a former controller-general:

> Until I held the post of Controller-General I would hardly believe that such a state existed. Believe it or not the French kingdom was ruled by thirty Intendants. Your parlements, Estates and Governors simply do not enter into the picture. (Tocqueville, 1856: 36.)

The system of intendants remained intact through the French Revolution. They emerged as "prefects" organized in a general administrative service which exercises executive authority in coordinating all other public instrumentalities in the French administrative system.

The constitution of OMB contains the necessary elements for the creation of a new Executive Service, apart from the Civil Service, analogous to the French administrative service. The Director of OMB is an equivalent of the old controller-general. The Washington-based coordinators are the intendants or prefects and super-prefects in a new executive service. A separate command structure responsive to presidential direction is interposed into the structure of other administrative services to assure that presidential instructions are effectively transmitted and enforced throughout the administrative apparatus. An executive service becomes the President's new management system—a duplicate chain of command—for attaining control over all levels of administration throughout the country.

If proposals by Congressman Henry S. Reuss to use revenue-sharing as a "catalyst" (i.e., a management tool) for reorganizing state and local governments (Reuss, 1970) and by James L. Sundquist to use presidential surrogates to coordinate intergovernmental relations were acted upon, we might contemplate that the new executive service would also become a command structure to "make federalism work" in a "coordinated" way. (Sundquist, 1969.) State and local authorities, as in the case of the French "parlements, Estates and Governors," would become the superfluous facade of government. In Bagehot's terms, they would become the "dignified" part of the government, distracting the attention and maintaining the allegiance of the uninformed masses while the "efficient" parts proceed with the actual work of government. (Bagehot, 1867: 59–65.)

A NEW SECRET POLICE?

A highly integrated executive structure where the power of command is fully centralized in a single Chief Executive will be subject to substantial problems of institutional weakness and institutional failure. *(Supra,* 58–64.) The creation of a duplicate command structure inherent in a specialized Executive Service as the equivalent of the French administrative service can attempt to overcome some of the impediment to communication and control. However, the personal costs associated with demands for action in accordance with Presidential instructions and orders can be expected to create resistance to executive authority. This resistance will become "one of the chief obstacles to effective government" centered in a fully integrated Chief Executive.

If a new executive establishment is to cope effectively with this obstacle it will become necessary to create a Special Investigations Unit to maintain executive secrecy

[143]

and to exercise discipline in relation to recalcitrant government employees. Efforts to tighten the screws of administrative control will cause bureaucratic pipelines to leak like sieves. Plumbers will be needed to stop the leaks. No chief executive can "master the Federal bureaucracy and make it do *his* will" (*Newsweek,* December 12, 1972, my emphasis) without access to new information systems. The new information system will require secret intelligence provided by secret police. Are the "plumbers" the beginnings of a new system of secret police?

Conclusion

The Reorganization Acts of 1939 and 1949 offer extensive opportunities for those who seek to strengthen Executive authority. They provide an Executive with substantial authority to legislate subject only to a sporadic legislative veto. Administrative organization is a key to control over the enforcement apparatus of government. Laws depend upon mechanisms for enforcement to become effective. Otherwise, laws are mere "words." If executive instructions can be interposed to direct enforcement practices apart from the prescriptions of general law, then executive instructions become effective law.

Reorganization Plan No. 2 thus contains the essential legal architecture for a radical alteration of the American constitutional system. Executive authority can displace congressional authority by substituting Executive instructions about *what* government should do. A system of administrative jurisprudence, based upon an additional reorganization plan, can be organized within the executive to displace judicial authority. Control over the essential functions of government can be encompassed entirely within the executive establishment. Thus, a new administrative state can be organized within the Executive Offices of the President. Among the essential elements for the governance of the new administrative state would be a National Security Council to assist the President in his responsibility for world affairs, a Domestic Council to assist the President to decide what government should do in domestic affairs, an Office of Management and Budget to assist the President in the management of internal affairs including interagency and intergovernmental relationships throughout the country, a Special Investigations Unit to provide the President with a secret information system so that he can eliminate obstacles to "effective" government, and, finally, a Council of State to adjudicate the grievances of citizens. The Executive Office of the President would then become the "efficient" part of the government; the Congress, the courts, the state houses, and the other centers of authority would become the "dignified" parts of government relieved of their other burdens of work so that they can devote themselves exclusively to the ceremonial functions of government.

If this vision of the strong Executive stirs misgivings among students and practitioners of public administration, we should give high priority to rethinking the intellectual grounds upon which the science and practice of public administration stands. A system of constitutional rule depends upon establishing limits to authority. Alexander Hamilton long ago recognized that strengthening the Executive implies that governments "acquire a progressive direction toward monarchy." (*Federalist* 8.) An unqalified concern for strengthening Executive authority will lead to absolutism and despotism. A passion for strengthening the Executive is inimicable to the survival of democratic institutions.

Watergate and the constitutional crisis of the 1970's are tragic experiences which suggest that the political theory upon which this country was founded can be ignored only at great risk. Americans confront the task of learning again how to use that theory as a tool for the analysis of policy problems and for the design of new institutions to cope with contemporary problems. (Bish, Ostrom, 1973.) That theory provides the basis for fashioning a system of democratic administration as an alternative to the omnipotent Executive functioning as a general manager over a fully integrated bureaucracy.

Notes

CHAPTER 1

¹A number of the essays in Merton's *Reader in Bureaucracy* reflect the experiences of social scientists with wartime bureaucracy. So do several of the case studies in Stein's *Public Administration and Policy Development*.

²Dwight Waldo has responded to my comment here by indicating:

> But what I meant to say, and still do vigorously contend, is this: *No* paradigm of a *disciplinary* nature can solve the problem. This because public administration is not a scientific discipline. It is a profession in a loose sense, a collection of related professions, which can, do, and must use paradigms, techniques, and so forth, from *many* disciplines.
>
> Put another way, if we need a paradigm it should be that appropriate to a profession rather than that appropriate to a scientific discipline. My historic analogy has been to "the medical profession;" I would qualify that nowadays by making my analogy "the health professions."

I am perfectly willing to accept Waldo's position on the assumption that problems of water-resource administration may require different bodies of knowledge from police administration, for example. Yet we are confronted with the question of whether such disparate fields of administration do face comparable organizational problems associated with externalities, common-property resources, and public goods. If so, there may be a general logic of collective action which is applicable to both types of problems.

[147]

[3]American Society for Public Administration, *News and Views,* 20 (October, 1970), p. 5.

[4]Niskanen (1971) indicates some of the differences that voting rules will have upon the expected output of public agencies. See generally his discussion in Chapter 13 and following.

CHAPTER 2

[1]Wilson also observes: "It is quite safe to say that were it possible to call together again the members of that wonderful Convention (of 1787) to view the work of their hand in the light of the century that has tested it, they would be the first to admit that the only fruit of dividing power has been to make it irresponsible." (Wilson, 1885:187.)

[2]So far as administrative functions are concerned, Wilson asserts "all governments have a strong structural likeness; more than that, if they are to be uniformly useful and efficient, they *must* have a strong structural likeness." (Wilson, 1887:218. Wilson's emphasis.)

[3]Wilson refers to a three-stage pattern of political development which he assumes to be applicable to the "chief nations of the modern world." These include: 1) a period of absolute rule, 2) a period of constitutional development, and 3) a period of administrative development. (Wilson, 1887:204.)

[4]Weber's theory of bureaucracy did not have substantial influence upon American study of public administration until after World War II when his translated work became available to American scholars. However, the generality of the Wilsonian paradigm is indicated by the congruence between Wilson's and Weber's formulations.

[5]The "monocratic principle" also implies "monopolization of legitimate violence by the political organization which finds its culmination in the modern concept of the state as the ultimate source of every kind of legitimacy of the use of physical force. . . ." (Rheinstein, 1954:347.) The persistent definition of political authority as a monopoly over the legitimate use of force indicates a monocratic or monocentric bias in modern political theory. Can a federal system with separation of powers be properly characterized as a "monopoly" over the legitimate use of force? I think not.

[6]Crozier (1964) in his chapter on "The Bureaucratic System of Organization" refers to Max Weber's place in the "paradoxical" view

of bureaucracy which runs through much of western political analysis. See the frontispiece for a statement of the "paradox."

[7]The disparity between Weber's conceptualization of bureaucracy as an ideal type of organization necessary for efficiency and for development of a rational basis for modern civilization and the consequences which he anticipates as following from its perfection in a "fully developed" form is difficult to fathom. He implies that a system of bureaucratic rule is necessarily the fate of modern man. He would thus affirm Rousseau's observation that "Man is born to be free but is everywhere in bondage." Such a conclusion is consistent with a "monocratic" or "monocentric" structure of political organization based upon a theory of absolute sovereignty. If all political authority resides in an absolute sovereign and if all others are equal in their state of subjection then Weber's conclusions follow. His portrayal of a "fully developed bureaucracy" is surprisingly congruent with Tocqueville's discussion of democratic despotism in the Fourth Book of Volume II of *Democracy in America*.

Bendix (1960) addresses himself to this anomaly in the concluding chapter of his biography of Weber. Bendix argues that Weber's concept of "bureaucracy under legal domination" must be distinguished from his political analysis of bureaucratization as a different type of intellectual exercise. (p. 456.) If we hold to Bendix's position, then bureaucracy as an ideal type assumes perfectly obedient functionaries. The maintenance of legal rationality does not follow except as it is postulated as a limiting condition in a logical exercise. If this is the case, then Weber fails to come to grasp with the problem of indicating the logically necessary conditions which will increase the probability that a political system will conduct its affairs in accordance with rules of law. As Bendix indicates, "Bureaucratization becomes compatible with a system of legal domination only if officials are prevented from usurping the political and legislative process." (p. 457.) But, what is to prevent officials from usurping the political and legislative process where a monopoly exists over the legitimate use of force? Thus, it is an open question whether bureaucratization is consistent with a rational legal order or whether bureaucratization is a prelude to human bondage. We shall return to this issue in the concluding lecture.

[8]Victor A. Thompson's *Modern Organization* (1961) is a major exception.

[9]This characterization of research in the "mainstream" of American public administration is largely associated with the administrative

survey movement. Shields' (1952) discussion of "The American Tradition of Empirical Collectivism" points to quite a different tradition of analysis. Shields summarizes this tradition in a concluding observation:

> The empirical collectivist assumes that collective action should be employed whenever necessary to solve public problems, but that the minimal action required to dispose of the problem should be undertaken. In considering a policy question, therefore, he concentrates his attention on the actual situation in an effort to fathom the all-important character of the problem and the conditions of its solution. His initial query is: is this a public problem? No *a priori* answer can be given to this question; the answer turns on the situation itself. If it is decided that the problem is of public concern, then his next question is: which agent of the community is best able to deal with this problem? Is a local private agency, a county board, a national private organization (such as the American Red Cross), a state bureau, or a national agency best suited? Again he must examine the problem situation to arrive at an answer. His final query is: What sort of action is required to dispose of the problem? Each possibility he must canvass, and on the basis of past experience and future expectations he must select the form of collective action which appears most appropriate. Questions such as these the empirical collectivist can feasibly discuss with his fellows. Their discussion can center on differences of opinion about actual situations, and these differences they can resolve by appeals to experience, by examining the evidence. Thus, they can arrive at propitious decisions regarding collective action, and can settle, in a democratic manner, policy questions. (pp. 117–118.)

Shields also indicates that "empirical collectivists" rely upon a " 'rule of economy:' the minimal action to dispose of a problem—and no more—should be undertaken collectively," and "that public action taken to dispose of a problem should redound to the benefit of the entire community." (p. 105).

Shields observes that "the empirical collectivist prefers voluntary to mandatory action, inducement to compulsion, restriction to prohibition. And if government action is required, he prefers public regulation of private enterprise to governmental operation of public enterprise." (p. 106.)

Finally Shields observes that the "empirical collectivist's" preoccupation with the welfare of the whole community leads him to take the point of view of the consumer: "The empirical collectivist is able to espouse the public interest as it is reflected in the welfare of citizens as consumers." (p. 105.)

[150]

The tradition of "empirical collectivism" is sharply at variance with the mainstreams of American public administration. Benjamin Franklin, Alexis de Tocqueville, and Frederick Jackson Turner reflect that tradition in their writing as do a variety of practicing administrators such as John W. Powell, Elwood Mead, and William Hammond Hall, and scholars such as John Dewey and Francis W. Coker. *None* of their works has come to occupy a position of central significance in the study of American public administration.

[10]The *Report* states, "In a democracy consent may be achieved readily, though not without *some* effort, as it is the cornerstone of the constitution." (p. 3, my emphasis.) By contrast "efficient management" is a matter of "peculiar significance."

Given the serious challenge to democratic government and constitutional rule being posed by the rise of totalitarian regimes during the 1930's, it is striking that the Brownlow Committee could so confidently dismiss considerations affecting "the consent of the governed" and the maintenance of constitutional rule. Such perspectives were congruent with their theory that the field of politics is outside a proper concern for administration. The commissioners apparently were not prepared to consider the possibility that a fully developed system of "efficient management" based upon their "canons of efficiency" could transform constitutional rule into a problematical condition.

[11]Simon (1952:1130) clarifies his distinction of "group," "organization," and "institution" in the following observation:

> In such a nest of Chinese blocks the smallest multi-person units are the primary groups; the largest are institutions ("the economic system," "the state") and whole societies. We will restrict the term "organization" to systems that are larger than primary groups, smaller than institutions.

[12]Where the amount of resources and the organization objectives are given, outside the control of the administrator, efficiency becomes the controlling determinant of administrative choice [within those constraints]. (Simon, 1947:122.)

[13]See the discussion of problems of institutional failure in "The Work of the Contemporary Political Economist." The tragedy of the commons, for example, can occur in the absence of appropriate institutional constraints. Thus, individualistic choice in the management of a common-pool resource where demand exceeds supply would lead to "irrational" behavior when viewed in relation to other decision making arrangements for the management of such resources.

[151]

CHAPTER 3

[1] Discussions of professionalism and bureaucratic organization often make a direct association between the two sets of phenomena. Thus, much of the discussion of professionalism among police is associated with centralization of authority and large-scale organization. However, professionalization can be treated as a separate variable from organizational structure. The practice of both medicine and law frequently occur in the context of relatively small organizations where relationships are organized through market-like transactions. Other professions such as the military are organized predominantly in large-scale organizations. If professionalization and organizational structure are treated as independent variables, we would expect quite different structures of opportunities to prevail among superintendents of schools and city managers than would exist in a highly bureaucratized structure such as the military service or the foreign service.

[2] Most of the political economists are associated with the Public Choice Society and publish a journal, *Public Choice*. Professor Gordon Tullock, Center for the Study of Public Choice, Virginia Polytechnic Institute and State University, Blacksburg, Virginia, is the editor of *Public Choice*.

[3] In taking the perspective of an "Omniscient Observer," an economist confines his use of an individualist calculus only to market structures and relies upon an assumption that general policies affecting social welfare can be determined by an omniscient and omnicompetent despot who can maximize social utility by taking account of all utility preferences. The assumption of perfect information used in formulating a model of perfect competition is essentially applied to the problem of collective choice made by a benevolent despot. Economists who use the analytical device of the Omniscient Observer find Hobbes' theory of sovereignty congenial for their purposes.

Most scholars in the Public Choice tradition prefer to apply an individualistic calculus to problems of collective choice where individuals have access to less than perfect information. Decision-making arrangements such as elections, representation, and legislation are mechanisms for translating individual preferences into collective choices.

[4] The classical theory of administration is essentially devoid of a theory appropriate to the analysis of problematical situations. Shields (1952) in his essay on empirical collectivists places substantial emphasis upon the structure of situations as providing the context

for conceptualizing policy problems. John Dewey (1927) defines a public as coming into being in an effort to control indirect consequences of action which impinge upon persons not directly involved. His concept is closely related to the concept of externalities used by the political economists.

[5]This position stands in contrast to Wilson's presumption that there is but one rule of "good" administration for all governments alike, or Weber's presumption regarding the technical superiority of bureaucracy over any other form of organization. (See Ashby, 1962.)

[6]This structure of relationships applies to air pollution, water pollution, the exploitation of fishery resources and many types of public facilities. The incentive for the individual is to take advantage of any opportunity available to him. If he does not, others will. Thus, the exploitation of a common-pool resource such as the whale stock in the world's oceans may proceed to a point where the species are exterminated. Short-term advantage deviates from long-term advantage. For people to take advantage of long-term opportunities requires a modification in decision-making arrangements so that the community of individuals involved can convert a negative-sum game into a cooperative or positive-sum game.

When the relevant field of effects includes a large number of small public jurisdictions with no overlapping jurisdiction capable of regulating the conduct of the several smaller ones relative to that field of effects, the tragedy of the commons can recur in competition among the several smaller jurisdictions. In the case of whaling, nation states may be too small for regulating the harvest of whales. Municipalities and counties may be inadequate units for dealing with problems of air pollution. Thus, Crozier (1964) is quite correct in indicating that the American political system is highly susceptible to institutional dysfunctions which he characterized as the "vicious circle of decentralization" (p. 236) and which I have followed Garret Hardin in calling "the tragedy of the commons."

A solution to such pathologies can be attained by seeking recourse to a larger jurisdiction which will bound the relevant field of effects. However, such solutions need not involve the creation of only one jurisdiction to the exclusion of all smaller jurisdictions. Reliance upon overlapping jurisdictions is an alternative mode of organization. Still another alternative would be to rely upon the decision-making capability of the next larger unit of government. Thus, reliance upon states to regulate interstate commerce will engender conflicts reminiscent of a negative-sum game. Federal authority to regulate interstate commerce will be essential to avoid destructive conflict among states. As economic relations became national in scope, increasing reliance upon Federal regulation was necessary for productive relationships. As economic relations become international in scope, we can contemplate a competitive rivalry among nations which can take on the characteristics of a negative-sum game. Appropriate solutions will require capabilities to take joint action at the international level.

[7]The concept of span-of-control, which was relied upon to explain hierarchical structures in the traditional theory of administration, implies a substantial limit to the capability of any one supervisor to exercise control over a number of subordinates. Tullock relies upon this limit to generate a theory of institutional weakness and institutional failure associated with bureaucratic organizations. The traditional theory of public administration failed to draw such inferences even though the substantial limits upon control were implied by the concept of span-of-control.

Simon pointed out that a loss of information and control would apply to the number of tiers in a hierarchical structure as well as the number of subordinates reporting to a single superior. Thus, increasing the number of tiers in a hierarchy would lead to a loss of information and control as between the top level of command and those at the lower echelons in any organization. Narrowing the command structure at each level of organization would lead to a loss of information and control by increasing the number of levels in an organization. Simon's formulation (Simon, 1947: 24–28) suggests serious limits to the aggregate size of a bureaucratic organization.

The elements for formulating a theory of institutional weakness and institutional failure applicable to bureaucratic organizations were inherent in the traditional theory of public administration; but the logic of that theory was not developed until Tullock's work. Weber anticipated the consequences but failed to provide the logical connection between conditions and consequences. Tocqueville in his *Old Regime and the French Revolution* (1854) provides us with an extended description of bureaucratic pathologies associated with a highly centralized political regime.

[8]The relationship of production of public goods and services to user preferences implies that various decision-making arrangements for articulating voter preferences and user demands have an essential relationship to administrative performance. Voting, representation, legislation, and the availability of various remedies for aggrieved users of public goods and services to enforce demands have significance

for administrative conduct. William A. Niskanen, Jr. (1971) has begun to explore these relationships.

Political economists would reject the presumption that public administration should be conceptualized apart from the political process inherent in the traditional dichotomy of politics and administration. Instead they would view various forms of voting, modes of representation, and rules for legislative action as critical processes for translating individual preferences into collective decisions to secure the provision of public goods and services. Thus, different voting rules will yield different outputs of public goods and services. In turn, they would also be concerned with the decision rules available to individual persons for invoking and enforcing demands for the provision of public goods and services. See my discussion of the "any-one rule" in *The Political Theory of A Compound Republic* (1971 a.)

[9]In fact, it is possible for an inappropriate tax policy to exacerbate problems of congestion in the long run rather than relieve them. G. S. Tolley (1969) argues that the use of federal funds to relieve congestion may have the opposite consequence. He argues that in such a situation, "the receiving entity will then have incentive to overspend. If large cities succeed in overspending relative to small cities, the tendency may be away rather than toward desirable city size." (p. 36.) In addition he argues that the "danger of overbuilding in large cities is heightened if facilities are built in response to projection of travel demands assumed to be independent of the effect of facilities themselves on city growth." Both factors when combined lead to a *cumulative* effect which moves in the *wrong* direction. *(Ibid.)*

[10]So far as I know, no literature by political economists addresses itself to the specific issue of authority regarding administrative reorganization. However, the Buchanan and Tullock (1962) analysis of decision rules would imply that reliance upon Presidential authority to formulate reorganization plans subject only to a Congressional veto is the equivalent of legislation by one-man rule subject to Congressional veto.

Reference to periodic needs to "shake up" the bureaucracy presumably implies deprivation costs for those who are shaken up. How do such experiences affect the productivity of the public service? This is the type of question that a political economist would be inclined to ask about the practice of administrative reorganization.

[11]The possibility of diversely structured systems of ordered relationships runs through the work of many different organization theorists. Ashby (1962) distinguishes among "fully-joined systems," "iterated

systems," and "multi-stable systems" and considers the relative adaptability of each. Christopher Alexander deals broadly with problems of organization and design in an article on "A City is Not a Tree" (1965a) and in *Notes on the Synthesis of Form* (1965b). Michael Polanyi in *The Logic of Liberty* (1951) explores the concept of polycentricity as the basis for spontaneous order as distinguished from hierarchy in a corporate order.

These different approaches to order have led to a consideration of whether an "invisible hand" operates in the public sector as well as the private sector. Lindblom (1959 and 1963), McKean (1965) and Bish (1968 and 1969) have advanced arguments on behalf of the invisible hand in government. Duggal (1968) challenged the contention. Tocqueville speaks of an invisible hand when he observes:

> Nothing is more striking to the European traveler in the United States than the absence of what we term the government or the administration. Written laws exist in America, and one sees the daily execution of them; but although everything moves regularly, the mover can nowhere be discovered. The hand that directs the social machinery is invisible. (Tocqueville, 1835 and 1840: I, 70.)

An invisible hand can become operable in the government of human affairs to the extent that bargaining, negotiation, and competitive rivalry can be used to regulate the conduct of diverse public enterprises in relation to one another. Thus, public universities govern relationships with one another through a variety of voluntary associations, contractual understandings, and forms of competitive rivalry rather than by reference to the command of superiors in an overarching bureaucracy.

[12]Daniel Elazar (1971) objects to the use of the term decentralization to refer to the authority exercised by smaller units of government in a federal system. He contends that decentralization implies an allocation of authority from the center by a superior authority to a subordinate set of authorities. Thus he argues that federalism implies "noncentralization" of authority. His argument is sound. A federal system necessarily implies overlapping jurisdictions and concurrent exercise of authority.

Lindblom (1965) makes a similar point in contrasting central and noncentral coordination.

CHAPTER 4

[1]Tocqueville used terms of "decentralized" as against "centralized" administration to refer to what conforms to Weber's distinction

between "democratic" and "bureaucratic" administration. Tocqueville's reference to centralization and decentralization are apt characterizations except for one unfortunate implication. Centralization is often juxtaposed to decentralization in the sense that we sometimes speak of centralization *versus* decentralization. The terms need not be mutually exclusive in a federal political system where several regimes coexist at different levels of government. The very structure of a federal political system implies overlapping jurisdictions and simultaneous reference to elements of both "centralization" *and* "decentralization." The characteristics that Max Weber identifies with democratic administration are precisely the characteristics that most impressed Tocqueville.

[2]Tocqueville conceptualizes a democratic society to be one where a strong equality of conditions exists among the people of such a society. He clearly recognizes that government in a democratic society requires radical conditions of inequality in decision making capabilities. Thus the disparity between the power of individuals living in a mass society and those vested with governmental prerogative in a highly centralized political structure is so overpowering that he despaired for the survival of liberty or free institutions in a centralized democratic society. He saw hope in the American system of overlapping jurisdictions and fragmentation of authority as permitting a sufficient dispersion of authority for freedom to exist in a democratic society. See especially Tocqueville's conclusions in the Fourth Book of Volume II of *Democracy in America*.

[3]It was these essays in particular that inspired Leonard White's historical studies in American national administration.

[4]Thus, politics cannot be viewed as *apart* from administration. Administrators as public servants or public employees are exposed to review and reconsideration of their decisions by other persons functioning in many different decision structures which occupy potential veto positions in relation to their decisions. An administrator selects his strategy in pursuing opportunities with an awareness that any act represents a move in a series of simultaneous games. If the game of administration is one dominated by an exclusive calculus of pleasing superiors, the consequences will be quite different than if public administrators stand exposed to the scrutiny of common councils representing citizens, to inquiries by grand juries, to actions by citizens in courts of law, to public scrutiny by a free press, as well as to the scrutiny of other executive officers and agencies.

[5]It is essential that we recall Tocqueville's definition of a democratic society as being one characterized by a condition of social and economic

equality. If we were to assume that greater social equality exists among members of Soviet society than in American society, then the Soviet Union would be a more democratic society than the United States by Tocqueville's definition. I have used Max Weber's defining characteristics for democratic administration to have the same meaning that Tocqueville used in defining "decentralized administration." Tocqueville would characterize the Soviet Union as a democratic society governed by a highly centralized administration controlled by an autocratic or self-perpetuating government.

CHAPTER 5

[1]Dwight Waldo in *The Administrative State* (1948) observes:

Influenced by British experience and British writers, Woodrow Wilson . . . and many others had contrasted our system of separation of powers unfavorably with cabinet government, and urged the need for stronger executive leadership. Students home from the Continent were anxious to find a formula that would enable democracy to secure the manifest advantages of autocracy. The traditional separation of powers became the *bête noir* of American political science, and exaltation of the powers of the executive branch its Great White Hope. (p. 36.)

[2]John Austin in *The Province of Jurisprudence Determined* (1832) formulates the concept of positive law as that which is enforceable. He argues that constitutional law, so-called, is positive morality not positive law. Austin's argument is consistent with Hobbes. However, Austin does not press his analysis very far in relation to the type of political structure represented by what he calls a composite state. See generally in his Lecture VI.

[3]A strong anti-legalist bias runs through the traditional study of American public administration. The problem of designing a political system which could enforce a system of constitutional law as against those who exercise the prerogatives of government is never considered. Wilson (1887) impatiently observed:

Once a nation has embarked in the business of manufacturing constitutions, it finds it exceedingly difficult to close out that business and open for the public a bureau of skilled, economical administration. There seems to be no end to the tinkering of constitutions. (p. 207.)

The efforts of other Americans to "tinker" with constitutions in the late nineteenth and early twentieth centuries could also be viewed as a critical factor in accomplishing reforms which substantially

[158]

reduced the opportunities for machine politics and boss rule. Among these modifications were the introduction of the Australian ballot, direct primaries, the initiative, referendum, and recall, the popular election of U. S. Senators, and other such measures.

Goodnow reflects the same bias in his reference to extra-legal institutions as though any undertaking not explicitly authorized in statutory law were extra-legal.

White (1948) also assumed that "the study of administration should start from the base of management rather than the foundation of law...." (p. xiii.) Yet paradoxically, White's writings drew heavily upon legal materials and public documents. Administration was still set upon a foundation of law but no effort was made to comprehend the relationship of administrative structures to the basic design of institutional arrangements in the American political system. Neither White, Goodnow, nor Wilson pondered the issue posed by Hamilton in the first paragraph of *The Federalist* where he raises the question, "Are societies of men really capable or not of establishing good government from reflection and choice, or are they forever destined to depend for their constitution on accident and force?" *(Federalist* 1. My transformation of an indirect question to a direct question.)

[4]Quoted by Alexander Bickel in a review of Gerald T. Dunne, *Justice Story and the Rise of the Supreme Court* in *New York Times Book Review,* May 30, 1971, p. 3.

[5]The discussion of "The Constitution of Self-Governing Public Enterprises" in the third lecture (pp. 78–84) is relevant for a consideration of constitutional decision making perspectives as against other political perspectives. Constitutional decision making according to Buchanan and Tullock (1962) is based upon "conceptual unanimity" and the relevant criterion for them is "Pareto optimality." Pareto optimality implies that those decision rules should be chosen which will lead to advances in human welfare in the sense that no one be left worse off.

John Rawls (1963, 1967) in a series of articles dealing with the criterion of justice as fairness suggests that the choice of decision rules be made on an assumption that each individual has an equal probability of being subject to decisions taken by his enemies rather than his friends. Rawls' criterion can be restated for students of public administration to contemplate the structure of organizational arrangements on an assumption that "bad guys" will occupy positions of authority as often as "good guys." If decision-making arrangements can be devised so that "bad guys" are exposed to a structural rig of the game where they are led to make reasonably good decisions, then we can expect some degree of success in devising appropriate organizational structures for human associations.

A person who invents a new game and expects that game to be successful must make certain assumptions about the capabilities of potential players and about fairness in the play of the game. Those who play the game select their strategies in order to win. The perspectives are quite different. However, if some set of players reach the conclusion that a game is structurally unfair, those who bear the burden of unfairness would rationally prefer not to play the game if they have a choice. Peasants through much of the world have long since learned that the political game is rigged against them.

The constitutional decision maker is concerned about the essential conditions of justice and fairness that apply to the rig of the game for collective decision making. The politician playing a particular election game, for example, is concerned with winning. The test of the appropriateness of a constitutional decision rule providing for popular elections is whether winning and losing over the long run without regard to particular politicians engenders the appropriate outcomes in assuring a just or fair allocation of resources in the provision of public goods and services.

Efforts to formulate legislation for the organization of water districts in California, for example, can be understood from a constitutional decision making perspective. (V. Ostrom and E. Ostrom, 1970.) One comes to quite different conclusions about the meaning of the California efforts using a constitutional decision-making perspective than most administrative analysts would in prescribing reorganization in accordance with the traditional principles of public administration.

[6]I deliberately chose to confine these lectures to the paradigm problem in *American* public administration. A problem of vastly different proportions would be raised if this discussion were extended to a comparative analysis of political systems and the reform of those systems. The existence of common assumptions that are relevant to the design of various types of political institutions implies that the development of a predictive political theory applicable to the study of different administrative systems is conceivable. The evidence of institutional weakness and institutional failure characteristic of large-scale bureaucracies is widespread. So is evidence regarding phenomena characteristic of the tragedy of the commons.

The much more difficult problem is whether reforms can be undertaken which will lead to the revolutionary transformation of one system into a different system based upon a radically different design. Changes in the structure of organizational arrangements cannot occur

[160]

independently of the political knowledge that is relevant to organizational practice among the persons involved. A system of bureaucratic administration cannot be transformed into a system of democratic administration except over a long period of time. Individuals in a society must acquire the knowledge, skills, and moral judgment that are necessary for undertaking joint efforts to realize common benefits. The work of Danilo Dolci is especially suggestive for students interested in this problem.

If 1) the scourge of war could be avoided on the European continent for several generations, 2) the European Community were able to negotiate a series of constitutional settlements where joint benefits (net after costs) accrue to all European peoples, and 3) appropriate European political structures were devised which permit the development of a European system of positive constitutional law, then I can imagine the gradual evolution of a system of democratic administration upon the European continent.

Revolutions like the Soviet Revolution do not represent basic changes in the constitutional structure of a political system. The Czarist state was destroyed, but the Soviet state has all the attributes of Hobbes' *Leviathan* with an absolute sovereign and a new elite to function as the ruling class. The major difference is that the Soviet state has fewer symptoms of bureaucratic senility than the Czarist state. Stalin's secret police were more rigorous and ruthless than their predecessors. Tocqueville's *Old Regime and the French Revolution* documents the continuity of French bureaucracy as the central feature of the French constitution through a period of revolutionary change. Crozier's *The Bureaucratic Phenomenon* substantiates its persistence to the present.

The task of fashioning political and administrative institutions for the so-called underdeveloped areas of the world is beyond the competence of American academicians. American academicians can contribute to a political science which others may then use in devising organizational arrangements which are appropriate to their entrepreneurial efforts. A political science can indicate considerations which are appropriate to an estimate of the opportunity costs inherent in different designs. Much of the literature on administrative development grossly underestimates the costs inherent in central planning and bureaucratic organization. No organizational arrangement will be cost-free.

[7]See for example the articles written by Albert Sigurdson in the Toronto *Globe and Mail,* December 30, 1970. Sigurdson writes that: "Security guard agencies are doing a $60 million dollar business in

Canada, double the level of five years ago, and new agencies continue to open across the country." Individuals are also investing heavily in private arms. A recent estimate made by the F.B.I. is that the "private arsenal in U.S. homes now totals 90 million weapons...." *(Newsweek,* August 17, 1970, p. 15.)

[8]The *New York Times* in an editorial on November 11, 1969 refers to a report which disclosed that two-thirds of the abandoned buildings being torn down as "unsafe" were structurally sound and probably capable of rehabilitation. If such an assertion is true, structurally sound buildings are being destroyed for failure to devise institutional arrangements with appropriate incentives for individuals to use and maintain the available housing stock.

[9]A reader of an earlier draft of these lectures raised the question: "Who are the 'individual persons' who form the 'relevant public' of a public administrator? For example, is it the duty of policemen to serve the criminals?" An answer to this question requires an evaluation of the community of persons potentially affected by "criminal" activity and a sense of moral judgment regarding the consequences following from such conduct. To judge unilaterally an act to be "criminal" is contrary to basic precepts of justice. Preliminary procedures are available to take action based upon a tentative judgment about the criminality of an act. Both the person who is suspected of being a criminal and the person who is convicted of being a criminal are entitled to be treated as individual persons in a democratic society.

Andrei Amalrik makes the essential point when he observes in *Involuntary Journey to Siberia* (1970) that:

> A court sentence ought not to be an act of vengence but the expression of a generally accepted idea of justice. The educational value of a trial lies in convincing the defendant and everyone else that he is being judged in strict accordance with the law and with the ethical standards that mankind has arrived at during its long history; it certainly does not lie in the Judge tediously haranguing the court or in his crudely defaming the defendant and witnesses. There is even less educational value in trials staged for avowedly propaganda purposes—as an object lesson to others. This in not a way of enlightening people but only of intimidating them, and it brings nothing but discredit upon the courts. When a man is charged with one thing but then accused of something else during the actual trial, this may help the police in achieving their limited aim, but it also results in still further deterioration of the whole system of justice. (pp. 112–113.)

If correctional administration is not oriented to the interest of individual persons who may have committed criminal acts, we can expect overwhelming failure in the administration of criminal justice.

[162]

Correctional authorities require a substantial sense of moral judgment in counseling and working with prison populations. People are more than obedient cogs in machines. The only way to remind ourselves of this moral imperative is to relate ourselves to the individuality of different persons. When that condition becomes impossible, moral conduct is no longer possible.

[10]As John Dewey once commented: "The man who wears the shoe knows best that it pinches and where it pinches, even if the expert shoemaker is the best judge of how the trouble is to be remedied." (Dewey, 1927:207.) He might have added that the man who wears the shoe is also the best judge of the appropriateness of the shoemaker's remedy.

POSTSCRIPT

[1]I am indebted to James Buchanan for suggesting that the implications of the intellectual crisis in American public administration be pursued in relation to the current constitutional crisis over executive authority. Dennis Smith and Philip Sabetti have been especially helpful in their critical comments and suggestions.

[2]I capitalize Executive when referring to the personification of the executive establishment in relation to the President as Chief Executive or as the "head" of that establishment.

[3]Max Weber in his discussion of domination refers to what he calls the "law of small numbers." (Rheinstein, 1954: 334.) A small ruling circle can easily dominate larger masses of people. The smaller the number of a ruling circle who have the capacity to command authoritative action, the greater the ease of pursuing preemptive strategies. A "monocratic" structure where "all functionaries are integrated in a hierarchy culminating in a single head" (Rheinstein, 1954: 334) has greatest advantage in pursuing preemptive strategies. Weber goes on to observe:

> Another benefit of the small number is the ease of secrecy as to the intentions and resolutions of the rulers and the state of their information; the larger the circle grows, the more difficult or improbable it becomes to guard such secrets. Wherever increasing stress is placed upon "official secrecy," we take it as a symptom of either an intention of rulers to tighten the reins of their rule or of a feeling on their part that their rule is being threatened. (Rheinstein, 1954: 334)

On the basis of the "law of small numbers," a President will always have a preemptive advantage in dealing with Congress. Congress can reduce the preemptive advantage of the President by assigning authority at the level where an agency is assigned responsibility to discharge public actions in terms of the standards of public law. The President can then discharge his executive responsibility to take care that "the laws be faithfully executed." Where all executive authority is vested in the President to command the entire executive establishment, his exercise of that authority will depend upon secrecy as to his intentions and resolutions. Such secrecy is inimicable to public accountability under rules of public and constitutional law in a democratic society.

List of References

Alexander, Christopher. (1964) *Notes on the Synthesis of Form.* Cambridge, Massachusetts: Harvard University Press, 1964.

――――. (1965) "A City is Not a Tree," *Architectural Forum,* 122 (April, 1965), 58–62, and *Ibid.* (May, 1965), 58–61.

Altshuler, Alan A. (1970) *Community Control: The Black Demand for Participation in Large American Cities.* New York: Pegasus, 1970.

Anderson, William. (1925) *American City Government.* New York: H. Holt and Company, 1925.

――――. (1942) *The Units of Government in the United States: An Enumeration and Analysis.* Chicago: Public Administration Service, 1942.

Arendt, Hannah. (1963) *On Revolution.* New York: The Viking Press, 1963.

Ashby, W. Ross. (1956) *An Introduction to Cybernetics.* New York: John Wiley & Sons, Inc., 1956.

――――. (1960) *Design For a Brain: The Origin of Adaptive Behavior.* Second edition. New York: John Wiley & Sons, Inc., 1960.

――――. (1962) "Principles of the Self-Organizing System," in *Principles of Self-Organization,* ed. by H. Von Foerster and G. W. Zopf. New York: The Macmillan Company, 1962. 255–278.

Austin, John. (1832) *The Province of Jurisprudence Determined.* H. L. A. Hart, ed. London: Weidenfeld and Nicolson, 1955. Originally published in 1832.

Ayres, Robert U., and Allen V. Kneese. (1969) "Production, Consumption and Externalities," *American Economic Review,* 59 (June, 1969), 282–297.

Bagehot, Walter. (1867) *The English Constitution.* R. H. S. Crossman, ed. London: C. A. Watts and Company, Ltd., 1964. Originally published in 1867.

Barnard, Chester I. (1938) *The Functions of the Executive.* Cambridge, Massachusetts: Harvard University Press, 1938.

Beck, Henry. (1970) "The Rationality of Redundancy," *Comparative Politics,* 3 (January, 1970), 469–478.

Bish, Robert L. (1968) "A Comment on V. P. Duggal's 'Is There an Unseen Hand in Government?'" *Annals of Public and Co-operative Economy,* 39 (January-March, 1968), 89–94.

————. (1969) "The American Public Economy as a Single Firm: Reply to Duggal," *Annals of Public and Co-operative Economy,* 40 (July-September, 1969), 361–365.

————. (1971) *The Public Economy of Metropolitan Areas.* Chicago: Markham Publishing Company, 1971.

————, and Vincent Ostrom. *Understanding Urban Government: Metropolitan Reform Reconsidered.* Washington, D.C.: American Enterprise Institute, 1973.

Blau, Peter L. (1956) *Bureaucracy in Modern Society.* New York: Random House, 1956.

Buchanan, James M. (1960) *Fiscal Theory and Political Economy.* Chapel Hill, North Carolina: The University of North Carolina Press, 1960.

————, and Gordon Tullock. (1962) *The Calculus of Consent: Logical Foundations of Constitutional Democracy.* Ann Arbor, Michigan: The University of Michigan Press, 1962.

————. (1966) "An Individualistic Theory of Political Process," in *Varieties of Political Theory,* ed. by David Easton. Englewood Cliffs, New Jersey: Prentice-Hall, Inc., 1966.

————. (1967) *Public Finance in Democratic Process: Fiscal Institutions and Individual Choice.* Chapel Hill, North Carolina: The University of North Carolina Press, 1967.

————. (1968) *The Demand and Supply of Public Goods.* Chicago: Rand McNally & Company, 1968.

————. (1969) *Cost and Choice: An Inquiry in Economic Theory.* Chicago: Markham Publishing Company, 1969.

————. (1970) "Public Goods and Public Bads," in *Financing the Metropolis,* ed. by John P. Crecine. Beverly Hills, California: Sage Publications, 1970.

Caldwell, Lynton K. (1965) "Public Administration and the Universities: A Half-Century of Development," *Public Administration Review,* 25 (March, 1965), 52–60.

Carey, William D. (1969) "Presidential Staffing in the Sixties and Seventies," *Public Administration Review,* 29 (September/October, 1969), 450–458.

————. (1970) "Remarks on Reorganization Plan No. 2," *Public Administration Review,* 30 (November/December, 1970), 631–634.

Christy, Francis T., Jr., and Anthony Scott. (1965) *The Common Wealth of World Fisheries.* Baltimore, Maryland: The Johns Hopkins Press, 1965.

Coase, R. H. (1937) "The Nature of the Firm," *Economica,* 4 (1937), 386–485.

Coker, F. W. (1922) "Dogmas of Administrative Reform," *American Political Science Review,* 16 (August, 1922), 399–411.

Committee for Economic Development. (1966) *Modernizing Local Government.* New York: Committee for Economic Development, 1966.

————. (1970) *Reshaping Government in Metropolitan Areas.* New York: Committee for Economic Development, 1970.

Crozier, Michel. (1964) *The Bureaucratic Phenomenon.* Phoenix Books edition. Chicago: The University of Chicago Press, 1964.

Cyert, Richard M., and James G. March. (1963) *A Behavioral Theory of the Firm.* Englewood Cliffs, New Jersey: Prentice-Hall, Inc., 1963.

Dales, J. H. (1968) *Pollution, Property and Prices.* Toronto: The University of Toronto Press, 1968.

Davis, Otto A., and Andrew B. Whinston. (1961) "The Economics of Urban Renewal," *Law and Contemporary Problems,* 26 (Winter, 1961), 105–117.

————, and ————. (1967) "On the Distinction Between Public and Private Goods," *American Economic Review,* 57 (May, 1967), 360–373.

Diamant, Alfred. (1962) "The Bureaucratic Model: Max Weber Rejected, Rediscovered, Reformed," in *Papers in Comparative Public Administration,* ed. by Ferrel Heady and Sybil L. Stokes. Ann Arbor, Michigan: Institute of Public Administration, The University of Michigan, 1962.

Dimock, Marshall E. (1937) "The Study of Administration," *American Political Science Review,* 31 (February, 1937), 28–40.

Downs, Anthony. (1957) *An Economic Theory of Democracy.* New York: Harper & Row Publishers, Inc., 1957.

————. (1967) *Inside Bureaucracy.* Boston: Little, Brown and Company, 1967.

Duggal, V. P. (1966) "Is There an Unseen Hand in Government," *Annals of Public and Co-operative Economy,* 37 (April-June, 1966).

Elazar, Daniel J. (1971) "Community Self-Government and the Crisis of American Politics," *Ethics,* 81 (January, 1971), 91–106.

Emmerich, Herbert. (1950) *Essays on Federal Reorganization.* University, Alabama: University of Alabama Press, 1950.

Feagin, Joe R. (1970) "Home Defense and the Police: Black and White Perspectives," *American Behavioral Scientist,* 13 (May/August, 1970), 797–814.

Follett, M. P. (1924) *Creative Experience.* New York: Peter Smith, 1951. Originally published in 1924.

[167]

Friesema, H. Paul. (1966) "The Metropolis and the Maze of Local Government," *Urban Affairs Quarterly,* 2 (December, 1966), 68–90.

Gerth, H. H., and C. Wright Mills, eds. (1946) *From Max Weber: Essays in Sociology,* Galaxy Book edition. New York: Oxford University Press, 1958. Originally published in 1946.

Goodnow, Frank J. (1900) *Politics and Administration: A Study in Government.* New York: The Macmillan Company, 1900.

Gordon, H. Scott. (1954) "The Economics of a Common Property Resource: The Fishery," *Journal of Political Economy,* 62 (April, 1954), 124–142.

Graham, F. P. (1968) "The Cop's Right (?) to Stop and Frisk," *New York Times Magazine,* December, 1968.

Gregg, Phillip M. (1972) *Reformulation of Theory in Policy Study.* Bloomington, Indiana: Indiana University, Ph.D. Dissertation, 1972.

Grodzins, Morton. *The American System.* Daniel J. Elazar, ed. Chicago: Rand McNally & Company, 1966.

Gulick, Luther, and L. Urwick, eds. (1937) *Papers on the Science of Administration.* New York: Columbia University, Institute of Public Administration, 1937.

Hacker, Andrew. *The End of the American Era.* New York: Antheneum, 1970.

Hamilton, Alexander, John Jay, and James Madison. (1788) *The Federalist.* New York: The Modern Library, [n.d.]. Originally published in 1788.

Hardin, Garrett. (1968) "The Tragedy of the Commons," *Science,* 162 (December, 1968), 1243–1248.

Hawley, Amos H., and Basil G. Zimmer. (1970) *The Metropolitan Community: Its People and Government.* Beverly Hills, California: Sage Publications, 1970.

Hayek, F. A. (1960) *The Constitution of Liberty.* Chicago: The University of Chicago Press, 1960.

Hirsch, Werner. (1964) "Local Versus Areawide Urban Government Services," *National Tax Journal,* 17 (December, 1964), 331–339.

————. (1968) "The Supply of Urban Public Services," in *Issues in Urban Economics,* ed. by Harvey S. Perloff and Lowden Wingo, Jr., Baltimore: The Johns Hopkins Press, 1968. 435–476.

Hirshleifer, Jack, James C. DeHaven, and Jerome W. Milliman. (1960) *Water Supply Economics, Technology, and Policy,* Chicago: The University of Chicago Press, 1960.

Hobbes, Thomas. (1651) *Leviathan or the Matter, Forme and Power of a Commonwealth Ecclesiasticall and Civil.* Michael Oakeshott, ed. Oxford: Basil Blackwell, 1960. Originally published in 1651.

Jacobs, Jane. (1961) *The Death and Life of Great American Cities.* New York: Vintage Books, 1961.

Knight, Frank H. (1921) *Risk, Uncertainty and Profit.* New York: Harper & Row Publishers, 1921. Reissued in 1965.

Kotler, Milton. (1969) *Neighborhood Government: The Local Foundations of Community Life.* Indianapolis: Bobbs-Merrill, 1969.

Kuhn, Thomas S. (1962) *The Structure of Scientific Revolution.* Phoenix Books edition. Chicago: University of Chicago Press, 1964. Originally published in 1962.

Landau, Martin. (1969) "Redundance, Rationality and the Problem of Duplication and Overlap," *Public Administration Review,* 29 (July/August, 1969), 346–358.

Leach, Richard H. (1971) "Federalism: Continuing Predicament," *Public Administration Review,* 31 (March/April, 1971), 217–223.

Lindblom, Charles E. (1955) *Bargaining: The Hidden Hand in Government.* Research Memorandum RM-1434-RC. Santa Monica, California: The RAND Corporation, 1955.

———. (1959) "The Science of 'Muddling Through'." *Public Administration Review,* 19 (Spring, 1959), 1–17.

———. (1965) *The Intelligence of Democracy: Decision Making Through Mutual Adjustment.* New York: The Free Press, 1965.

Llewellyn, K. N., and E. A. Hoebel. (1941) *The Cheyenne Way: Conflict and Case Law in Primitive Jurisprudence.* Norman, Oklahoma: University of Oklahoma Press, 1941.

Long, Norton E. (1952) "Bureaucracy and Constitutionalism," *American Political Science Review,* 46 (September, 1952), 808–818.

———. (1969) "Reflections on Presidential Power," *Public Administration Review,* 29 (September/October, 1969), 442–450.

———. (1970) "Rigging the Market for Public Goods," in *Organizations and Clients: Essays in the Sociology of Service,* ed. by William R. Rosengren and Mark Lefton. Columbus, Ohio: Charles E. Merrill Publishing Company, 1970.

McConnell, Grant. (1966) *Private Power and American Democracy.* New York: Alfred A. Knopf, 1966.

McKean, Roland N. (1958) *Efficiency in Government Through Systems Analysis, With Emphasis on Water Resource Development.* New York: John Wiley & Sons, Inc., 1958.

———. (1965) "The Unseen Hand in Government," *American Economic Review,* 55 (June, 1965), 496–506.

Mansfield, Harvey C. (1969) "Federal Executive Reorganization: Thirty Years of Experience," *Public Administration Review,* 29 (July/August, 1969), 332–345.

March, James G., and Herbert A. Simon. (1958) *Organizations.* New York: John Wiley & Sons, Inc., 1958.

Margolis, Julius. (1955) "A Comment on the Pure Theory of Public Expenditures," *Review of Economics and Statistics,* 37 (November, 1955), 347–349.

Martin, Roscoe C. (1952) "Political Science and Public Administration," *American Political Science Review,* 46 (September, 1952), 660–676.

Mayo, Elton. (1933) *The Human Problems of an Industrial Civilization.*

New York: The Viking Press, 1960. Originally published in 1933.

Meehan, Eugene J. (1971) *The Foundations of Political Analysis, Empirical and Normative.* Homewood, Illinois: The Dorsey Press, 1971.

Merton, Robert K., Ailsa P. Gray, Barbara Hockey, and Hanan C. Selvin, eds. (1952) *Reader in Bureaucracy.* New York: The Free Press, 1952.

Millett, John D. (1959) *Government and Public Administration.* New York: McGraw-Hill Book Company, 1959.

Mishan, E. J. (1969) "The Relationship Between Joint Products, Collective Goods, and External Effects," *The Journal of Political Economy,* 77 (May/June, 1969), 329–348.

Niskanen, William A., Jr. (1971) *Bureaucracy and Representative Government.* Chicago: Aldine-Atherton, 1971.

Olson, Mancur. (1965) *The Logic of Collective Action.* Cambridge, Massachusetts: Harvard University Press, 1965.

———. (1969) "The Principle of 'Fiscal Equivalence': The Division of Responsibility Among Different Levels of Government," *American Economic Review,* 59 (May, 1969), 479–487.

Ostrom, Elinor. (1968) "Some Postulated Effects of Learning on Constitutional Behavior," *Public Choice,* 5 (Fall, 1968), 87–104.

———. (1971) "Institutional Arrangements and the Measurement of Policy Consequences: Applications to Evaluating Police Performance," *Urban Affairs Quarterly,* 6 (June, 1971), 447–475.

———, Roger Parks, and Gordon Whitaker. (1971) "The Effect of Size and Community Control on the Provision of Police Services: A Comparative Study of Three Independent Communities and Three Matched City Neighborhoods Within One Metropolitan Area," Prepared for presentation at the meetings of the Public Choice Society, Blacksburg, Virginia, April 22–24, 1971.

———, and ———. (1971b) "Black Citizens and the Police: Some Effects of Community Control," Prepared for presentation at the annual meeting of the American Political Science Association, Chicago, September 7–11, 1971.

———, William Baugh, Richard Guarasci, Roger Parks, and Gordon Whitaker. (1973) *Community Organization and the Provision of Police Services.* Beverly Hills, Calif.: Sage Publishers, 1973.

———, and Gordon Whitaker. (1973) "Does Local Community Control of Police Makes a Difference? Some Preliminary Findings," *American Journal of Political Science,* 17 (February, 1973).

Ostrom, Vincent. (1968) "Water Resource Development: Some Problems in Economic and Political Analysis of Public Policy," in *Political Science and Public Policy,* ed. by Austin Ranney. Chicago: Markham Publishing Company, 1968.

———. (1969) "Operational Federalism: Organization for the Provision of Public Services in the American Federal System," *Public Choice,* 6 (Spring, 1969), 1–17.

————. (1971a) *The Political Theory of a Compound Republic: A Reconstruction of the Logical Foundations of American Democracy as Presented in The Federalist.* Blacksburg, Virginia: Virginia Polytechnic Institute, Center for Study of Public Choice, 1971.

————. (1971b) *Institutional Arrangements for Water Resource Development,* PB 207 314. Springfield, Virginia: National Technical Information Service, 1971.

————, and Elinor Ostrom. (1965) "A Behavioral Approach to the Study of Intergovernmental Relations," *Annals of the American Academy of Political and Social Science,* 359 (May, 1965), 137–146.

————, and ————. (1970) "Conditions of Legal and Political Feasibility," in *Natural Resources Systems Models in Decision Making,* ed. by Garrett H. Toebes, Lafayette, Indiana: Purdue University, Water Resources Research Center, 1970. 191–208.

————, and ————. (1971) "Public Choice: A Different Approach to the Study of Public Administration," *Public Administration Review,* 31 (March/April, 1971), 203–216.

————, Charles M. Tiebout, and Robert Warren. (1961) "The Organization of Government in Metropolitan Areas: A Theoretical Inquiry," *American Political Science Review,* 55 (December, 1961), 831–842.

Parsons, Talcott, ed. (1947) *Max Weber: The Theory of Social and Economic Organization.* New York: The Free Press, 1964. Originally published in 1947.

Polanyi, Michael. (1951) *The Logic of Liberty: Reflections and Rejoinders.* Chicago: University of Chicago Press, 1951.

Press, Charles. (1963) "The City Within a Great City: A Decentralist Approach to Centralization," *Centennial Review,* 7 (1963), 113–130.

Rawls, John. (1963) "Constitutional Liberty and the Concept of Justice," in *Nomos VI: Justice,* ed. by Carl J. Friedrich and John W. Chapman. New York: Atherton Press, 1963. 98–125.

————. (1967) "Distributive Justice," in *Philosophy, Politics and Society,* ed. by Peter Loslett and W. C. Runciman. Oxford: Blackwell and Sons, 1967. 58–82.

Reuss, Henry S. *Revenue-Sharing: Crutch or Catalyst for State and Local Governments?* New York: Praeger Publishers, 1970.

Revel, Jean-Francois. (1971) *Without Marx or Jesus, the New American Revolution Has Begun.* Garden City, New Jersey: Doubleday & Co., 1971.

Rheinstein, Max, ed. (1954) *Max Weber on Law in Economy and Society.* A Clarion Book edition. New York: Simon and Schuster, 1967. Originally published in 1954.

Ridley, Clarence E., and Herbert A. Simon. (1938) *Measuring Municipal Activities; A Survey of Suggested Criteria and Reporting Forms for Appraising Administration.* Chicago: The International City Managers Association, 1938.

Riggs, Fred W. (1968) "The Crisis of Legitimacy: A Challenge to

Administrative Theory," *Philippine Journal of Public Administration*, 12 (April, 1968), 147–164.

Samuelson, Paul A. (1954) "The Pure Theory of Public Expenditure," *Review of Economics and Statistics,* 36 (November, 1954), 387–389.

Shackle, G. L. S. (1961) *Decision, Order and Time in Human Affairs* Cambridge, England: Cambridge University Press, 1961.

Shields, Currin V. (1952) "The American Tradition of Empirical Collectivism," *American Political Science Review,* 46 (March, 1952), 104–120.

Simon, Herbert A. (1943) *Fiscal Aspects of Metropolitan Consolidation.* Berkeley, California: University of California, Bureau of Public Administration, 1943.

——. (1946) "The Proverbs of Administration," *Public Administration Review,* 6 (Winter, 1946), 53–67.

——. (1947) *Administrative Behavior: A Study of Decision-Making Processes in Administrative Organization.* New York: The Free Press, 1965. Originally published in 1947.

——. (1952) "Comments on the Theory of Organizations," *American Political Science Review,* 46 (December, 1952), 1130–1139.

——. (1957) *Models of Man: Social and Rational; Mathematical Essays on Rational Human Behavior in a Social Setting.* New York: John Wiley & Sons, 1957.

——. (1959) "Theories of Decision Making in Economics and Behavioral Science," *American Economic Review,* 49 (June, 1959), 253–283.

——. (1960) *The New Science of Management Decision.* New York: Harper & Row, 1960.

——. (1965) *The Shape of Automation for Men and Management.* New York: Harper & Row, 1965.

——. (1969) *The Sciences of the Artificial.* Cambridge, Massachusetts: The M.I.T. Press, 1969.

——, William R. Divine, E. Myles Cooper, and Milton Chernitz. (1941) *Determining Work Loads for Professional Staff in a Public Welfare Agency.* Berkeley, California: University of California, Bureau of Public Administration, 1941.

Stein, Harold. (1952) *Public Administration and Policy Development: A Case Book.* New York: Harcourt & Brace, 1952.

——. (1963) *American Civil-Military Decisions: A Book of Case Studies.* University, Alabama: University of Alabama Press, 1963.

Stigler, George S. (1962) "The Tenable Range of Functions of Local Government," in *Private Wants and Public Needs: Issues Surrounding the Size and Scope of Government Expenditure,* ed. by Edmund S. Phelps. New York: W. W. Norton, 1962.

Sundquist, James L., with the collaboration of David W. Davis. (1969) *Making Federalism Work: A Study of Program Coordination at the Community Level.* Washington, D.C.: The Brookings Institution, 1969.

―――. (1970) "Organizing U.S. Social and Economic Development," *Public Administration Review,* 30 (November/December, 1970, 625–630.

Thompson, James D. (1967) *Organizations in Action.* New York: McGraw-Hill Book Company, 1967.

Thompson, Victor A. (1961) *Modern Organization.* New York: Alfred A. Knopf, 1961.

Tiebout, Charles M. (1956) "A Pure Theory of Local Expenditure," *Journal of Political Economy,* 44 (October, 1956), 416–424.

Tocqueville, Alexis de. (1835 and 1840) *Democracy in America.* Two volumes. Phillip Bradley, ed. New York: Alfred A. Knopf, 1945. Originally published in 1835 and 1840.

―――. (1856) *The Old Regime and the French Revolution.* Doubleday Anchor Books edition. Garden City, New Jersey: Doubleday & Company, Inc., 1955. Originally published in 1856.

Tolley, G. S. (1969) *The Welfare Economics of City Bigness.* Urban Economics Report No. 31. Chicago: The University of Chicago, 1969.

Toulmin, Stephen E. (1961) *Foresight and Understanding, An Enquiry into the Aims of Science.* Bloomington, Indiana: Indiana University Press, 1961.

Tullock, Gordon. (1965) *The Politics of Bureaucracy.* Washington, D.C.: Public Affairs Press, 1965.

―――. (1969) "Federalism: The Problem of Scale," *Public Choice,* 6 (Spring, 1969), 19–29.

―――. (1970) *Private Wants, Public Means: An Economic Analysis of the Desirable Scope of Government.* New York: Basic Books, Inc., 1970.

United States Codes, Congressional and Administrative Laws. 91st Congress, Second Session, 1970. Vol. 3. St. Paul, Minn.: West Publishing Company, 1971.

U.S. Congress, Joint Economic Committee, Subcommittee on Economy in Government. (1969) *A Compendium of Papers on the Analysis and Evaluation of Public Expenditures: The PPB System.* Three volumes. Washington, D.C.: U.S. Government Printing Office, 1969.

U.S. President's Committee on Administrative Management. (1937) *Report With Special Studies.* Washington, D.C.: U.S. Government Printing Office, 1937.

Vile, M. J. C. (1967) *Constitutionalism and the Separation of Powers.* Oxford: The Clarendon Press, 1967.

Wagner, Richard E. (1971) *The Fiscal Organization of American Federalism: Description, Analysis, Reform.* Chicago: Markham Publishing Company, 1971.

Waldo, Dwight. (1948) *The Administrative State: A Study of the Political Theory of American Public Administration.* New York: The Ronald Press Company, 1948.

―――. (1955) *The Study of Public Administration.* New York: Random House, Inc., 1955.

————. (1968) "Scope of the Theory of Public Administration," in *Theory and Practice of Public Administration: Scope, Objectives, and Methods,* ed. by James C. Charlesworth. Philadelphia: The American Academy of Political and Social Science, 1968. 1–26.

Walters, A. A. (1961) "The Theory in Measurement in Private and Social Cost of Highway Congestion." *Econometrica,* 29 (October, 1961), 676–699.

Warren, Robert O. (1964) "A Municipal Services Market Model of Metropolitan Organization," *Journal of the American Institute of Planners,* 30 (August, 1964), 193–204.

————. (1966) *Government in Metropolitan Regions: A Reappraisal of Fractionated Political Organization.* Davis, California: Institute of Governmental Affairs, University of California, 1966.

————. (1970) "Federal-Local Development Planning: Scale Effects in Representation and Policy Making," *Public Administration Review,* 30 (November/December, 1970), 584–595.

Wengert, E. S. (1942) "The Study of Public Administration," *American Political Science Review,* 36 (April, 1942), 313–322.

Weschler, Louis F., and Robert Warren. (1970) "Consumption Costs and Production Costs in the Provision of Antipoverty Goods," Paper delivered at the sixty-sixth annual meeting of the American Political Science Association, Los Angeles, California, September 8–12, 1970.

White, Leonard D. (1939) *Introduction to the Study of Public Administration.* Revised edition. New York: The Macmillan Company, 1939.

————. (1948) *Introduction to the Study of Public Administration.* Third edition. New York: The Macmillan Company, 1948.

Wildavsky, Aaron. (1966) "The Political Economy of Efficiency," *Public Administration Review,* 26 (December, 1966), 292–310.

Wilson, Woodrow. (1885) *Congressional Government: A Study in American Politics.* New York: Meridian Books, 1956. Originally published in 1885.

————. (1887) "The Study of Administration," *Political Science Quarterly,* 2 (June, 1887), 197–220.

Index

[177]

cept of organization, 44–45; theory of organization, 11, 18
Social pathologies, 3, 4, 113
Social production functions, 18, 45
Sovereignty, 100–102; Hobbes' theory of, 107, 109; Unitary, 101, 105
Span of control, 34; principles of, 38, 117
Special Investigations Unit, 135, 143
Spill-over effects, 54
Stein, Harold, 9
Stigler, George S., 119, 120
Structure of events, 52–54, 64
Sundquist, James L., 122, 143
Theory of a firm, 47
Theory of bounded rationality, 46
Thompson, James D., 45
Tiebout, Charles M., 61, 70, 72, 118, 121
Tocqueville, Alexis de, 21, 79, 80, 81, 91–97, 106–107, 113, 142
Traditional or classical theory of administration, 5, 9, 10, 11, 17, 18, 19, 20, 26, 36, 49, 73, 74, 82
Tragedy of the commons, 56–58, 62, 64, 69, 126
Transaction costs, 59
Tullock, Gordon, 60, 66–67, 70, 116, 118, 120, 131
Uncertainty, 51, 105
Unitary or monocentric state, 85

Unity of command, 7, 34, 37, 41, 45, 78; principle of, 41–42
U. S. President's Committee on Administrative Management, 35, 41
Urwick, L., 6, 20, 36, 37, 38, 39, 40, 41, 42, 48, 122, 131
Value-free social science, 8
Veto positions, 89
Vile, M. J. C., 103
Voting rule, 68
Wagner, Richard E., 72
Waldo, Dwight, 10, 11, 18
Warren, Robert O., 61, 70, 72, 118, 121
Watergate, 134 ff.
Weber, Max, 8–9, 10, 20, 29–33, 61, 77–79, 80, 81, 89, 93, 96, 97, 128; theory of bureaucracy, 8, 20, 29–33, 163
Wengert, E. S., 24
Weschler, Louis F., 61
Whinston, Andrew, 53, 126
Whitaker, Gordon, 118
White, Leonard D., 7, 24, 49–50, 131
Wildavsky, Aaron, 50
Willoughby, 131
Wilson, Woodrow, 9, 20, 21, 23–29, 30, 33–34, 35, 48, 74, 75, 76, 79, 81, 95, 98, 100, 102, 110, 131, 133; theory of administration, 26–29, 35, 37, 96, 110, 133; Wilsonian paradigm, 28–29, 34, 114, 137–38
Zones of authority (zoned authority), 44, 59